HUNTING *in the* LAKE DISTRICT

HUNTING in the LAKE DISTRICT

SÉAN FRAIN

MERLIN UNWIN BOOKS

First published by Merlin Unwin Books, 2010

Published by:
Merlin Unwin Books
Palmers House
7 Corve Street
Ludlow
Shropshire SY8 1DB
U.K.

www.merlinunwin.co.uk

Designed and set in Bembo by Merlin Unwin
Printed in England by Cromwell Press Group

ISBN 978-1-906122-23-2

CONTENTS

Glossary of hunting terms   9

1. A typical day's hunting   13

2. Origins and development   18

3. The structure of a fell pack   51

4. D'ye ken John Peel?   72

5. Lake District Shepherds' Meets   91

6. Hunting the fox   105

7. Hunting the hare   155

8. Crag-fast   170

9. Hunting the otter and the mart   179

10. Hounds and terriers of the Lake District   191

11. Hunting the fells today   210

To that unknown hunter
from Lincolnshire

ACKNOWLEDGEMENTS

Many thanks to all the kind and generous Cumbrian folk who have contributed so much valuable material for this book, including Gordon Bland, Maud Vickers, Pearl Wilson, Gary Middleton and Dick Peel. Also, many thanks to Gordon and Mary Martin, keen Blencathra followers, and the management at the Bridge Hotel, Buttermere, the Pheasant Inn, Wythop, and the Borrowdale Hotel, Borrowdale Valley, for allowing me to make copies of old and rare photographs of fell hunters from past generations.

The dramatic photo on the front cover of a fox and hounds at 'the dungeon' on Helm Crag at Grasmere was taken by professional photographer Neil Salisbury who runs the Betty Fold Gallery and Tea Room near Ambleside (see www.bettyfold. co.uk, telephone 015394 36611).

GLOSSARY OF HUNTING TERMS

Bay, to: This is when a terrier barks at a fox in order to bolt it, or guide the diggers. Hounds also bay, or 'give tongue' either whilst hunting a line, or marking an earth. To 'stand at bay' is when the fox turns and faces the hounds at close quarters.

Bield: or borran. A naturally formed rock-pile. This term is used exclusively in the Lake District.

Bink, to: When a fox crawls onto a narrow ledge on a steep crag in order to escape hounds, it is said 'to bink'.

Bobbery pack: A scratch hunting pack of local dogs including hounds, terriers, lurchers, sheepdogs.

Bolt, to: When a fox leaves its earth and makes for the open ground, usually after a terrier has been sent in, though foxes have been known to bolt when hounds mark and dig at an earth.

Borran: A naturally-formed rock-pile, as opposed to a man-made pile found in many old quarries. Borrans often cover a vast area and are very deep. They are incredibly dangerous places in which to enter a terrier.

Bothy: A simple mountain hut in a remote area, often stone built, offering shelter to shepherds or anyone lost overnight on the mountains and fells.

Brock: Colloquial for a badger.

Brush: Colloquial term for the tail of a fox. These are like a bottle-brush and come in a range of colours and sizes, some with large white tips, others without. Some are even black.

Cast: Hounds fan out and test the ground for scent.

Charlie: Colloquial term for a fox, thought to originate from the MP Charles James Fox. Foxes are sometimes also referred to as 'Charles James', or 'Reynard', or Tod.

Check: Temporary loss of scent.

Cold drag: Old scent, which is followed by hounds even though the quarry is no longer there.

Coupled: When terriers are shackled together using a small length of chain known as Couplings. These help keep terriers under control, preventing the risk of them sheep worrying and the possibility of a terrier sneaking off to go down a nearby earth when its owner isn't looking. Hounds are also coupled at times, especially youngsters. These are chained to older, wiser hounds (trenchers) who teach them manners and respect for livestock. Couplings, however, do not prevent two terriers from getting stuck in an earth, so vigilance is required

Covert: Woodland or under-growth in which foxes spend daylight hours.

Den: The underground home of a fox – *see also* Earth.

Drag: The scent of the quarry, or the line (route) it has taken

Draw, to: When the Huntsman takes his hounds in search of a fox, they are said to 'draw' a Fellside, for example, or under crags. They run around, searching for a scent trail (a line). Huntsmen draw all the most likely places.

Earth: A fox's underground den.

Entered to fox: When a hound or terrier, on reaching maturity, is used for the hunting of foxes. Once a hound or terrier has 'served its apprenticeship' and is now working foxes, either hunting their line or going into fox earths, they are said to be entered to fox.

Fell, a: A moor, or mountain. This term is used in the Lake District, North Yorkshire and North Lancashire in particular.

Find, to: When hounds 'find' it means they have encountered the skulking/resting fox and made it move from its hiding place. A terrier is said 'to find' when it stops running and begins baying at its fox, which is usually trapped in at this point.

Fresh fox: one that jumps up as another is being hunted, and leads the hounds away, acting as a diversion or decoy, sometimes splitting the pack.

Gather, to blow the: When the Huntsman blows a set series of notes on his horn to call back the hounds, this signals the end of hunting for the day. It can take some time for the hounds to return when the Gather is blown and sometimes hounds remain missing overnight if they have gone miles adrift from the pack. The Huntsman will search for missing hounds for hours, often until darkness falls.

Ghyll: Pronounced 'gill'. *See also* Gryke. A deep ravine which usually carries a mountain stream down to the valley bottom. Some ghylls are very steep and nigh-on impossible to cross.

Ground, go to: When a pursued fox no longer feels safe fleeing above ground, he heads into an earth in order to escape the hounds. This is when the terriers take over. They are entered either solely or as a couple, in order to either bolt or kill the fox underground. The latter is particularly preferable if the fox is a lamb- or poultry-killer. It requires a great deal of skill for the terrier to kill a fox which has gone to ground. To avoid injury, the terrier has to try for a throat-hold, throttling the fox and cutting off its air supply.

Gryke: *see also* Ghyll. A gryke is a fissure or crack in the crag face or outcrop of rocks.

Harrier: Slower hound with good scenting abilities; halfway in size between a beagle and a foxhound.

Huntsman: In the Fell country the Huntsman is appointed by the Hunt Committee to look after hounds and kennels, feed them, keep their environment clean and in good repair and treat minor ailments or injuries. The Huntsman is often the sole person employed, in which case his job can include the role of Kennelman, Whipper-in and terrierman. In Willie Irving's day, however, a Whipper-in was usually employed to assist the Huntsman, both while out hunting, and back at the kennels. The Huntsman is paid during the hunting season only (September to around the middle of May).

Line, a: A scent trail, or a 'drag'. When hounds suddenly get on the scent of a fox and start following it as one, instead of all fanning out, this is called hunting a line.

Made worker: Refers to a hound or terrier which is so experienced that it can be relied upon to do its job without any further training.

Marking: When hounds indicate that a fox is in the hole below, by scratching and baying.

Master of Foxhounds (MFH): The Master oversees the running of the pack of hounds and helps the committee to organise hunting and social events, as well as liaising with farmers and landowners. This is an important, hands-on post and the MFH is heavily involved in the day-to-day running of the hunt.

Meet, a: The place where hunt staff, followers, hounds and terriers gather at the start of the day's hunting. Hospitality is usually enjoyed, with tea, coffee, whiskey and brandy often supplied before the start. Afterwards, a social evening at the same venue is sometimes held, or the night before, where drink and food such as a traditional tattie pot (a kind of stew) is enjoyed. Pub games, dancing and sing-songs are the norm. All the different hunts have their own particular songs, though some are universal such as 'Joe Bowman'.

Puppy walking: When weaned, young hounds are 'farmed out' to hunt supporters, often farmers and villagers, to be raised, socialised, and familiarised with livestock and other dogs, so that they are already well behaved when they start hunting. These hounds then go back to live with the same families when the hunting season ends each year, leaving the Huntsman and Whip to find employment elsewhere. It is a great service to the hunt, as the puppy walkers personally fund the care of the hounds while they have them.

11

Puss: Affectionate nickname for a hare. A hunted hare is always referred to as a female.

Reynard: Term for a fox, also known as 'Charlie'. The word 'Reynard' derives from the French word for fox: 'renard'.

Run down, to: To catch a fox on open land, in other words to exhaust and out-manoeuvre it, often after a lengthy hunt.

Semi-trencher-fed: A pedigree hound, raised as a puppy by a local, and boarded by them out of the hunting season, but given back to the pack for kennelling throughout the hunting season.

Trail hunting: A trail of scent laid, either using aniseed, or scent from the bodies of foxes flushed and shot in order to control their numbers. Special trail hounds race across the fells, following this previously-laid drag.

Trencher-fed: A pedigree hound, which lives full-time with a local person, all year round, who brings it to the pack on a hunting day.

Tufter: A hound used to find and flush a fox from a covert or from undergrowth.

Typey: Refers to a terrier; handsome, good-looking, of good conformation.

Whipper-in: The assistant to the Huntsman on hunting days, as well as in the general care of the hounds at the kennels. The Whip will often climb out higher than the Huntsman and watch out for a fox leaving its chosen lair as the hounds draw across a Fellside. A Whipper-in must be as fit and keen as the Huntsman and his role is just as important although few packs have the funds to employ a professional Whip these days.

Worry, to: To kill a fox by throttling and shaking it; either below ground using a terrier or above ground using the hounds.

The fox has no natural predator but man. Without hunting, there would be no incentive to tolerate, let alone preserve, any fox. Hunting gives the fox worth in the fells. The result is wholly good: a stable, tolerable population of healthy foxes managed by an exhilarating activity which is the centre of a way of life.

Submission on behalf of the Central Committee of Fell Packs to the Committee of Inquiry into Hunting with Dogs

1

A TYPICAL DAY'S HUNTING

Hunting in John Peel country, around the wild and bleak Caldbeck Fells, hounds drew on for some time and distance and the chances of rousing a fox grew slim, as winter days were short up on the high grounds and an early beginning to a hunt was much preferred. Douglas Paisley, the honorary Whipper-in of the famed Blencathra Foxhounds, had climbed out to the higher places while the Huntsman, George Bell, traversed the lower slopes, cheering on hounds as they fanned out across the hillsides and cast at every likely spot.

They made their way carefully across scree, rockpiles and bields, they plunged through deep heather and gorse, searching every nook and cranny below the high, jutting crags. The huge bulk of the Skiddaw and Blencathra mountain ranges loomed menacingly over the proceedings as Reynard was sought throughout the forbidding and rough landscape where the winds were fit to 'blow yer 'ead off'.

After much ground had been covered, Douglas Paisley finally stumbled on a fox lying at the head of Roughton Ghyll and Silver Ghyll and there at last he laid hounds on. He cheered them on eagerly and the whole pack almost burst their hearts trying to come together and join the front runners who were now speaking keenly, their swelling chorus sweeping across the broad wild moorland, reaching right up to the high places from

Watching the hunt on the hill behind Thirlmere: a young 'Pritch' Bland (2nd from right, later to become Master of the Melbreak), his mother Mary Bland (far left), Bill Bland (6th from left), Sally, sister of Mary, (7th from left – she married the Huntsman Johnny Richardson.

where it resounded time and again amongst the broad, sheer-drop crags.

Paisley had out with him his strain of Kennel Club winning pedigree Lakeland terriers and their steel coupling jangled as they followed on the heels of their master in keen anticipation of what lay ahead. This bleak landscape is full of boggy peatland, deep heather, scree, rock and tall crags and is rough indeed. John Peel hunted here too, often abandoning his fell pony and taking to his feet when the going was bad. Wide rivers also made keeping up with hounds an additional challenge in this area and sometimes, if a bridge wasn't nearby, there was no choice but to wade in order to stay in touch.

Paisley was a fit man and he kept in touch as best he could, as the Blencathra pack settled to the line and followed their 'pilot' who took them over some of the roughest ground in the Lake

District, going by Haysghyll and to the heights of High Pike behind Skiddaw, amidst hidden valleys, ghylls and crags, where hounds had hunted foxes on thousands of occasions throughout several generations.

Reynard now crossed the high country and made for Carrock Pike, an area whose peat earths could be deadly to any terrier put to ground there. He had several earths from which to choose as the hounds began to press him hard, but he made for a rocky spot instead and just reached a deep and dangerous borran, known locally as Hammer Hole, before hounds could overtake him. He crept among the boulders lying one on top of another and skulked about the deep, dark refuge in the hope of evading detection.

However, Paisley was soon up with his terriers and a brace were loosed into the earth, one of which was probably Blencathra Punch, a well-bred pedigree Lakeland sired by Dick of Cogra and borne by Tess, possibly the bitch bred out of Joe Wilkinson's Deepdale Holloa and Willie Irving's famous and incredibly hardy Gypsy of Melbreak. Gypsy was not only a looker, but a first-rate worker who once bolted a fox from a deep rock earth on Robinson Fell above Buttermere, only to follow her fox out onto a dangerous crag where the tough terrier lost her footing and fell some distance down the sheer rock face. She was badly injured, but thankfully she made a full recovery and served for several more seasons with the Melbreak Hunt.

Gypsy was a granddaughter of G.H. Long's wonderfully game dog, High Lea Laddie. Blencathra Punch was one of Paisley's best at the time and was such a good worker, having been used at fox, badger and otter, that Willie Irving brought him into his own strain of pedigree Lakeland terrier and used his progeny with the Melbreak pack. It is likely that Tess was Irving's bitch, as many of the stud dogs he used were related to his original bloodlines and he frequently bred related stock in order to retain and improve the desirable qualities that made them winners in both the show ring and the hunting field.

Two terriers were put into Hammer Hole that day simply because it was so vast an area, not to mention deep, and the game pair searched through the rockpiles eagerly, thoroughly, their noses guiding their every movement, pushing their elusive quarry along the labyrinth of passages and finally pinning down their foe, despite this earth having a bad reputation as an 'impossible' place.

Foxes had not only refused to be shifted from this place during past forays with the hunt, but they had also been so elusive that terriers sent in to bolt them often couldn't pin them down. Sometimes a terrier was judged as not being able to find underground after emerging without anything to show for their

Walter Parkin with the Lunesdale hounds in 1951 (see page 48).

efforts, but often the problem was that the earth was so big that Reynard couldn't be pushed into a suitable dead-end and just continued to give the poor little tyke the run-around. On this particular day, Reynard wasn't for facing hounds in the open again and so the brave Punch and his companion worried their fox below ground and the carcass was later 'grubbed' out ('dug out' in fell parlance) by those keen and determined followers

The day had begun in rather poor fashion, but things had picked up and a second fox was soon roused by hounds and run to earth in similar fashion to the first. This fox was also 'worried in' by the terriers and a second dig soon uncovered the dead quarry, before approaching darkness made getting off the fell imperative. It had been a good day for the Blencathra Foxhounds, despite an unpromising start, and turned out to be a typically difficult, though exciting and productive day for hounds, terriers and foot followers alike. In fact, it had developed into a typical day with a Lake District Fell Pack.

2

ORIGINS & DEVELOPMENT

The origins of fell hunting are ancient and shrouded in mystery but it is certain that early hunting was carried out in order to control predator numbers. These predators will have preyed on livestock reared for the survival of early settlers, and allowing predator numbers to grow would have meant, in the end, that rearing such livestock successfully would have become impossible. Foxes, badgers, otters, polecats, pinemartens, stoats and rats were all on the quarry list and these were hunted purely as a means of protecting livestock, probably until the reign of Elizabeth I when an Act of Parliament passed laws protecting grain which offered bounties for every fox or badger killed. These bounties extended to most other predators in Cumbria in particular and some of these payments were quite lucrative. And so the killing of predators in the Lake District became quite a profitable venture, until the bounty system ended around the end of the 19th century.

Early settlers

From the earliest settlements of the Lake District, the communities there have been incredibly tight-knit. Evidence suggests that early settlers remained mainly around the coastal districts of Cumbria, but they did take advantage of the mountainous areas for essential supplies, especially around Langdale where hard

Blencathra foxhounds (see page 39) outside the Borrowdale Hotel with Huntsman George Bell (holding terriers) and Whip Albert Benson (left).

rocks were used for making tools such as axes and agricultural implements that could be employed for planting seeds etc. The Cumbrian coastal regions provided fertile land for crop growing and grazing livestock, while the sea obviously provided fresh food that was readily available to any brave enough to venture out in hand-made boats which were sturdy and buoyant enough to cope with often rough conditions.

The mountainous areas were not inhabited significantly until the coming of the Vikings, though it wasn't directly from Norway that these peoples came. It is thought that many of the early Viking settlers to Cumbria arrived via Ireland and the Isle of Man and that by this time they were second or even third generation, having been absorbed by the Celtic race. Possibly they were heading to the mountainous areas of Cumberland in order to flee from yet more Viking raids under King Harald.

The Vikings were a mountain race and would not have feared the innermost parts of the Lake District as had their predecessors.

Until the spirit of tourism took hold centuries later, during the eighteenth century (after 1769 in particular when Thomas Gray explored the innermost parts of the fells and dales and wrote of his discoveries) most explorers had a great fear of going into the mountains, some even believing that dragons and other monsters inhabited such regions and guarded those hidden mountain passes against any who tried to go there. But the Nordic/Celtic people felt at home among the mountains and they were specialist farmers, able to scratch a living from the poorest soil and they were sheep herders of great skill. It was probably these settlers, or their descendants, who established a breed of sheep able to survive in the harshest of terrain: this strain became the Herdwick breed which we know today.

These Norsemen also left us with enchanting names that make the Lake District unique and 'fell', 'dale' and 'thwaite', common names in mountainous country, originated from the Norse language. Indeed, it seems that many of our mountainous areas, including the Yorkshire Dales and the Derbyshire Peak District, attracted Nordic settlers who were able to make much better use of the often poor ground for farming.

It was probably these settlers, Vikings infused with Celtic blood, who first brought hounds and terriers to the mountainous areas of what we now know as the Lake District. The Celts were a great hunting race and historical evidence proves they bred and used both hounds and terriers during their forays in search of game.

Although the Romans came to the Lake District, they seem to have made little impact there, except maybe for some quarrying activity for slate and rocks which were used for building purposes, and it seems they mostly stuck to the perimeters of this region.

It was during the twelfth century that the Normans arrived in the area, but they too seemed to have kept mainly to the outskirts where they built several castles and attempted to keep

Lunesdale hounds waiting for a bolt.

law and order by containment, rather than conquest. Already the Cumbrian race was tight-knit and fiercely defended its lands, so conquest seems to have had little impact there, though through the centuries several communities did experience problems from raiding Scotsmen.

The Normans were also a great hunting race and undoubtedly brought in particular hounds to Cumberland. The descendants of the already-established Irish hounds were probably crossed with the French hounds and such breeding, I believe, became the foundation for the modern Fell Foxhound, which is a distinct breed from the Standard English Foxhound.

Some believe that miners from Holland and Germany brought the first hounds with them from the sixteenth or seventeenth century onwards and that these were the foundation for the Fell Foxhound. But that doesn't take into consideration the massive impact Irish Norsemen and Norman settlers had already had on the hunting scene of this area. The Dutch and German settlers no doubt did import hounds and possibly terrier-like dogs too and these, in time, once the new arrivals had been absorbed into the local population (there were hostilities between the indigenous and immigrant miners for many years), would have had an influence on future breeding policy, contributing to what eventually became the Fell Foxhound and the Fell, or Lakeland, terrier. But there were many strands, I believe, in the mix.

Bounty hunters

Because high bounties were offered on many predators, professional pest controllers were attracted to the area from Scotland and from possibly Ireland too, from Elizabethan times onwards. These bounty hunters brought hounds, terriers and running dogs with them and such were used as teams in the Highlands and Lowlands of Scotland to great effect at fox, badger, otter and several other predator species. Hounds were used to hunt and locate quarry such as foxes, while terriers were used to flush them from earths, or dense undergrowth.

The running dogs were there to catch the fleeing quarry as quickly as possible. This was about control and claiming bounties, not about long hunts and great hound work. Where running dogs could not be used, such as high on rocky mountainsides strewn with boulders and scree, guns were later employed and large numbers of predators were accounted for using such methods. So effective were these methods that foxes were incredibly scarce, even extinct it was reported, in some parts of Scotland. The Scottish Todhunters, as they were known, brought their methods to the fell country of the Lake District and, I believe, had a massive impact on future hunting.

The Lake District Fell Packs, however, were organised on an unusual basis, perfected by the region's own iconic Huntsman, John Peel (1777-1854), who perfected the cost-effective method of the semi-trencher-fed pack, kennelling the hounds during the hunting season, then sending them back to their owners during the summer. The original owners, who would be local farmers and labourers, would have been given the hounds as puppies to bring them up until they were old enough to hunt, and they would give them back to the hunt during each season.

Until around the time of John Peel, hunting with hounds had been slow and methodical and, when the lair of a fox, or polecat, or badger had been reached, terriers were put in and the bolting quarry shot, or if the quarry refused to bolt, very often it was dug out. These early hounds up to the 1700s were probably too slow to catch many foxes and otters, so shooting and digging out was the preferred method.

However, when foxhunting took off in a big way from the 1800s, the emphasis shifted to having great sport. The gentry began to take more of an interest in hunting on the fells and faster hounds were required. It seems likely that earlier slow hounds were crossed with running dogs, probably those brought to Cumberland by the Todhunters, and breeding from such crossbred stock eventually gave rise to the Fell Foxhound. This would explain why Fell Foxhounds are faster and lighter of bone than other hunting hounds.

Running dogs would be at great risk of breaking their legs on the fells of the Lake District and so a strong, but fast, hound became the ideal. So the slower hounds were crossed with such running dogs as greyhounds, deerhounds or lurchers. These crossbreds could be most useful and there is an interesting tale of when a lurcher and a foxhound from the Lunesdale kennels accidentally mated (I am sure the pair involved didn't view it as an accident!) and a hunt follower kept one of the pups, which grew into a superb worker.

One day hounds were hunting a fox in the Mallerstang district and the Lunesdale pack were gradually gaining ground as they stuck doggedly to the line. However, the follower with the hound/lurcher cross was out that day and his dog slipped its leash, ran ahead of the pack rather swiftly and pulled down the fox in double-quick time, much to the annoyance of Huntsman and field, who accused him of slipping the dog and asked him not to bring it along again.

The Blencathra, near Whinlatter in 1966, celebrating Johnny Richardson's 20th year with the hunt (see page 40).

But before foxhunting took a real hold in the fells in Georgian times, there were more packs of harriers, than there were foxhounds. A harrier is a hound, in size, half way between a foxhound and a beagle, and these harriers were quite a bit slower than foxhounds. Earlier harrier blood was used to endow the modern strains of fellhounds with strong scenting genes, and the ability of steadily following a trail: ideal for pursuing the hare, which was the favoured quarry up to Peel's time.

Many of these early harrier packs were infused with foxhound blood, some from the Shire packs, in order to create a better foxhunting hound for the fells. Neil Salisbury's fascinating book *The History of the Coniston Foxhounds* confirms that the Coniston pack originally hunted hare as their principal quarry and that the pack mainly comprised harriers. True, they also hunted fox when they could be found, but they usually failed to catch them until foxhound blood was introduced to the Coniston pack.

Development of the fellhounds from harriers

Today's harriers, which until the Hunting Ban were still used to hunt the hare, tend to be light and lean and very fast, but the harrier of yesteryear was more heavily built and slow – a methodical worker that could stick to a line for hours and out-manoeuvre the hare by exhausting it, in much the same way as packs of wolves will hunt deer for long periods and successfully make the kill when exhaustion overcomes the quarry.

The old harrier blood could only have been useful for infusing better scenting qualities and not for speed, and this was their contribution to the specialist Fell Foxhound we know and love today.

I have a copy of an old newspaper article from the late nineteenth century which possibly sheds light on the more recent history and development of the Fell Foxhound. The article is an interview with Squire Benson who, from 1865, was the owner and, together with R. Mitchell, the joint Master of the Melbreak Hunt.

He states that there were once white and black hounds, quite fast in their work, found throughout the fells, until a vagrant hunter arrived on the eastern side, bringing with him a small pack of hounds that were to have quite an influence on future breeding policy. That vagrant hunter reputedly arrived via Lincolnshire and was probably a travelling professional pest controller heading to where paid bounties were highest. And there was no more prosperous place for bounties than the Lake District at one time. Many pest controllers earned much of their living in this way, supplemented with farmwork; and several of these bounty hunters eventually settled in the Lake District and took small farms for themselves.

This chap came to the fells with hounds and possibly a few rough-and-ready terriers too and Squire Benson stated that those hounds were incredibly good workers, though quite a bit slower than the new, faster ones by then being worked in the fells. Benson also told the journalist interviewing him that those hounds were blue mottled and that they came to be known as 'Frain' hounds, probably named after the chap who first took them to the fell country. The Frain hound was crossed with the faster Fell Hound for one reason only: its excellent scenting ability.

[This is obviously of great personal interest to myself, as this chap may well have been one of my ancestors. The name Frain has its origins in the Norman family of De Freyne who settled

Johnny Richardson, Huntsman of the Blencathra, and Stan Mattinson near Mill Inn, Mungrisedale.

in Ireland and who became Masters and Huntsmen of several packs of hounds which hunted deer, then fox when deer were in short supply. It is my belief that the blue mottled hounds that arrived via Lincolnshire were bred down from French hounds, which is where the blue colouring originated and which is still found on some French hounds today. Possibly this travelling pest controller originally brought them to Cumbria from Ireland, sometime during the late eighteenth, or very early nineteenth, century. Our family 'legend' states that our ancestors came to England via County Cork and it is interesting to note that the Freeney family, the name derived from De Freyne, settled in Cork and there are still several families of this name in that area. The name of Frain came from Freeney and families of this name have settled all over the world after the mass emigration that resulted from the potato famine of the 1840s.]

So the hounds that arrived with this vagrant were more heavily-built and slower than those already being used in Cumberland, but their excellent scenting abilities made a vast impression with local hunters and were brought into local strains of hounds, particularly in the eastern fells where the different packs were eventually brought together to form the Ullswater and Blencathra Foxhounds.

Benson stated that those slower but harder hunting blue-mottled hounds had little impact on western packs, but many

The Ullswater pack meet at Patterdale in 1907. Note the coupled terriers in the foreground right, one of which is Ullswater Turk.

of the best hounds from eastern packs have been used as studs all over the Lakes country, just as the best of the western packs were used in the same manner. The diverse influence from those hounds of old has been felt throughout the whole of the Lake District and beyond. True, this cross might have slowed down the Fell Foxhounds for a time, which had in the preceding decades been purposely bred to be fast enough to quickly pull down foxes, otters, pinemartens and polecats, in order to claim as many bounties as possible, but the Frain hounds' ability to scent made them worthwhile additions to the mix.

As we move towards the 1900s, more emphasis was given to hound work and longer hunts, so these hounds, with vastly improved noses thanks to the 'Frain' hound influence, became well-suited to those developing tastes in which much more enjoyment was being had from the sport of watching hounds work out long drags and then, after rousing quarry, hunting it over many miles. Squire Benson used hounds from the east to bring into his privately-owned Melbreak pack. He stated that he used studs from Patterdale; as well as from Coniston and Wasdale. He also stated that he brought in blood from Lord Leconfield's West Sussex pack, which may well have influenced the Blencathra pack too.

It is interesting to note that by the latter half of the nineteenth century, the Melbreak terriers were predominantly 'reddish, strong-haired and courageous'. Squire Benson stated that three were sadly lost when put in at a fox at Brunt Bield, above Butter-mere, which had been driven in by hounds. This red colouring has long been associated with Irish terriers that came to the Lakes with Irish labourers and farm workers, as well as immigrants escaping famine. This article gives us a fascinating insight into the history of Fell Foxhounds and hunting in the English Lake District.

Douglas Paisley with the Blencathra hounds at St John's in the Vale. The hounds are obviously busy working out the line.

Origins of the Melbreak, the oldest Fell Pack

Squire Benson also left us a valuable record of how the Melbreak first came into existence. The early history of this famous pack resembles that of the Blencathra Hunt.

A hundred years ago a hound was kept at nearly every farmstead in the Lake District and whenever a fox was causing havoc amongst the sheep-folds and hen-roosts, a meet would be arranged. This was called a 'trencher-fed pack'. Each farmer came, attended by his faithful hound, and in the wild chase that ensued over craggy peaks and yawning chasms, the red robber had an exceedingly hot time of it.

By 1807, something like an organised pack, consisting of some six or seven couple, existed under the Melbreak Mastership of Mr William Pearson of Bannock, to whom they belonged. Mr John Hudson of Ullock succeeded him and was master for about forty years. Then Mr John Nicholson of the Hill held office until 1865, when Messrs. John Benson and R. Mitchell of Cockermouth acquired the pack and managed it together. John Benson kept the hounds practically as his own private property, for subscriptions in those days were few and far between.

The Melbreak is reputed to be the oldest of all the fell packs and it is believed that some of their blood goes back to the hounds of old John Peel. This is likely, as Peel had a hard-working and successful pack, noted for their ability to work out a scent for hours at a time, and such hounds would be natural studs for other packs.

There is likely to be some blood of Peel's hounds in all of the fell packs, but mostly in the Blencathra and Melbreak Hunts.

Squire Benson

This newspaper article tells us something of Squire Benson himself, stating:

'Mr Benson is probably one of the most extraordinary hunters in the British Isles. Though a solicitor in practice at Cockermouth, he yet actively fulfils the duties of Master of the Melbreak Hounds during the winter half of the year, while in the summer months he is just as indefatigable in the pursuit of the otter with the West Cumberland Otter Hounds, of which he is Master, with a small subscription. A peep into his sanctum at his residence in Cockermouth suffices to give a good idea of the man and the hobby. The walls of the apartment are covered with paintings of hounds – foxhounds and otterhounds – and a large bookcase contains nearly every work of authority on field sports in general.

'The master himself looks a typical hunter. He is a wiry, well-made man, his frame burdened with no useless weight, sound in wind and limb. In all that concerns hunting he converses as one speaking with authority. He is particularly strong on the question of breeding hounds.'

This is a fascinating insight into one of the Melbreak's most famous of sporting Masters. Squire Benson was something of a celebrity in his day and he was celebrated, as many Masters and Huntsmen were, in song and rhyme. It could well be stated, in fact, that his passion and drive in the hunting field would easily have rivalled that of John Peel, and John Benson should go down in the annals of hunting history alongside Peel, Bowman, Dobson and Willie Porter.

Benson hunted hare, otter and fox with his hounds, as well as any pinemartens they could find (the latter were already scarce by that time). He boasted that his hounds, although quite able to follow the line of a range of quarry, would only hunt one exclusive line at a time. If hare was the quarry, they would only hunt hare; if fox was on the list for that day, then they would only hunt fox; and the same with otters and pinemartens.

Two songs are of particular interest and both were composed by Edward Nelson of Gatesgarth. The Nelson family have farmed in the Lake District for generations and they were noted Melbreak supporters, walking hounds and terriers for the hunt, as well as breeding their own strain of what was then known as Patterdale terriers.

Edward Nelson was born in 1846 and died in 1934, and the two songs he composed are as follows:

Come all ye keen hunters while I relate
Of a fox chase that was run of late
By the Melbreak Hounds with their usual skill
Determined, if they find, to either hole or kill.

Squire Benson with Huntsman, hounds and horn
At the early dawn on a frosty morn
To Brackenthwaite Fells he did repair
Where Sir Reynard had been taking his Christmas fare.

To the top of Hobcarton they dragged him on high
And into Gasgale Crags where bold Reynard did lie
He was aroused from his slumbers by Jack Pearson's view holloa
Made his coat stand on end as the hounds they did follow.

By Whiteside and Grasmoor he took them several rounds
Closely pursued by those gallant 'laal' hounds
Over Lanthwaite Green and on past Scale View
Where he bid his old native land a fond adieu.

Then up Low Bank and through Buttermere
Men, women and children did give him loud cheer
As they crossed the Dubs at Crummock Lake Head
The cry was enough for to waken the dead.

Through Buttermere Scale near to Scale Force
They made bold Reynard for to change his course
He climbed Red Pike above Bleaberry Combe
Where the echo told him plain that death was his doom.

Over High Stile summit and on past Brunt Bield
Through Burtness Combe they forced him to yield
With hunters, hounds and fox in view
They did him in gallant style pursue.

Then down in the intacks of Gatesgarth Farm
They drove poor Reynard in great alarm
And in Burtness Close near by the lakeside
They pulled him down on the plain so wide.

With sixteen hounds and terriers four
They soon made Reynard for to breathe no more
And those who had joined the chase in their clogs
Did loudly give praise to those Loweswater dogs.

It was Christmas Eve in the year '69
So we did repair to the Fish Inn and dine
With the spirits we did make them fly in their pace
In fine chorus with this glorious race.

So fill up a bumper and we'll all have a horn
And drink success to the next hunting morn
For of all the sports that I ever did see
Chasing the fox is the best one for me.

On the 10th day of March in the year 1879
The Melbreak Hounds were uncoupled, the morning proved fine
Up Hope Ghyll, in Brackenthwaite, at the head of Lorton Vale
Where the music soon re-echoed over mountain and dale.

Chorus (repeated after each verse):
Tally-ho, tally-ho, hark forrard good hounds, tally-ho.

Right up to Hobcarton they dragged him along
Then to Gasgale Crags where his highness did be
And he being aroused by Pearson's view holloa
Bank's cried, "Hark to Singwell" and the rest in chorus did follow.

Round Whiteside and Grasmoor he led them a dance
At Thornthwaite and Braithwaite he took but a glance
To be chased in the lowlands he did not intend
So away to Addacombe Top, by Eel Crags did ascend.

Wandope and Addacombe he left in the rear
And crossed Newland Hause above fair Buttermere
But landscapes and scenery to him had no charm
As he hied over Robinson, above Gatesgarth Farm.

By Dale Head and Yew Crags his course he did steer
Where he passed Will Rigg and John Nelson,
                              who loudly did cheer
Saying, "Of our lambs and fat geese thou shalt have no more,"
"I can try", says bold Reynard, "as I oft did before."

The grand echoes of Honister, to him were revealed
As he clamb out Grey Knotts of Gillicombe Bield
Through by Ennerdale Head his course he still led
O'er the summit of Gable, to try Wasdale Head.

Through all his long life, he had never led such a trail
And he found his old limbs were beginning to fail
But he didn't call at Will Ritson's for refreshments or guide
But to view Scawfell Pike he onward did hie.

From Eskdale to Langdale he returned with a rush
With five gallant hounds running close to his brush
They passed by John Dawson, descending the Sty
Who, following, exclaimed, "Those hounds they can near fly."

Borrowdale Church his next intent was to reach
And there no doubt he'd have made his last speech
But his bloodthirsty followers would not allow him that berth
So they ran him in the open and put him to death.

He proved a fine dog fox, the King of his tribe
But could not save his life by either fair means, nor bribe
His estates no doubt will be left to his heir
And as for his old widow, well, she must claim her own share.

Thanks to our Borrowdale friends for their kindness shown
In taking care of our hounds when hunters were thrown
After four hours' fast running, the like never been seen
O'er snow mounted heights and townships thirteen.

Success to John Benson, his hunters the same
For his well cared-for hounds bring honour to his name
Though they're few in number, they're second to none
And the pride of the county to which they belong.

Goodwill while hunting, there is plenty for all
As hounds in other boundaries occasionally fall
But do unto others as you would they do unto you
And with good fellowship I will bid you adieu.

Johnny Richardson, Blencathra Huntsman (front row 3rd left) and Joe Wear (3rd right) at the Rydal Hound Show, 1963.

The best hunt of Squire Benson

Squire Benson witnessed some truly long hunts and one of the best occurred in the 1860s, after a meet at Gatesgarth, where the Melbreak Hunt continues to meet to this day. Hounds picked up a drag soon after being loosed at Warnscale Bottom, which took them over Fleetwith and onto Gillicombe borran where a fox was marked in (ie the hounds indicated that it had entered there, by baying and scratching) and left to ground (undisturbed), this being a bad spot. A bad spot is usually one in which terriers had been lost in the past, such as an underground gryke (hole), or some dangerous underground cavern where perhaps a wily fox would get on an underground ledge and leave the terrier to plunge to its death.

Next, hounds were taken up towards the Honister district and were soon away on another drag, unkennelling their fox at Buck How, which in those days was known as Buckstones How.

Reynard took them towards Newlands Head and on to Yew Crag, where he binked (sheltered on a ledge), but was turned out after much effort by the followers and hunt servants, with Willie Clark using his whip to move Reynard on.

Charlie now made for Honister quarry and the slate workers cheered on hounds as they attempted to keep on his line in this incredibly rough area. He now took hounds onto Fleetwith and kept to the high places, taking in Great Gable and Kirkfell, after crossing the heights of wild Grey Knotts. Lilter and Briton led the pack, their voices swelling and echoing amongst the high crags of this remote and bleak area and the pack fairly flew as they dropped down into the low country and crossed the river Liza, now making out for the Black Sail district.

The fox turned back for Kirkfell and climbed out for Gable again, which he ran round three times, before making for Sty Head Tarn. Rally and Ruffler now led the pack and they were taken all the way back to Gillicombe and on to Brunt Scarf borran (marked on the map as Burnt Scarth) where Reynard went to ground, with Lively, Ruffler, Rally and many others scratching at the unyielding rock in an attempt to reach him.

Huntsmen were quickly on the scene and four terriers were put into this huge place. Merry, Dandy, Grip and Wisp searched among the rocks and Merry, it seems, was first up, taking a bit of a mauling before Reynard was finally accounted for; worried in the earth and dug out by the eager followers, which included Edward and George Nelson.

This mammoth hunt was celebrated in song, and Mitchell and Benson received much praise for the efforts of this gallant pack. Christopher Bland, the son of Richard 'Pritch' Bland and grandson of Harry Hardisty, hunted the Melbreak while also working as a full-time shepherd at Buttermere. At a tragically young age, Christopher died in the year this book went to press, 2010, following a short illness, and he is greatly missed.

The Blencathra has its origins in several small trencher-fed packs originally kept by farmers, and the trencher-fed Keswick hounds feature particularly strongly in their early history. In 1826 Squire Crozier took ownership of the pack, kennelling them at Threlkeld. They were originally known as the Threlkeld Hounds, but became fondly nick-named 'Squire Crozier's Hounds'. Crozier knew John Peel and may have used his stud hounds, or taken drafts from him.

He also bought some of Peel's best hounds after his death in 1854, Briton and Cruel among them, and the pack then became known as 'the John Peel Hunt' and retain that nick-name to this day. The Threlkeld Hounds became a subscription pack in 1870 (ie were kennelled and paid-for by membership fees), and Squire Crozier remained Master until his death in 1903. I have seen a stuffed fox caught by Crozier's pack during the nineteenth century. The label stated that the fox was one of the old 'greyhound' variety, reputed to be larger, more cunning and with far more strength and stamina than a 'normal' fox [more of 'greyhound' foxes later].

And this fox may well have been the one that was roused one day on Skiddaw and went on to give Crozier's renowned pack a mammoth run that took in the vastness of the Borrowdale Valley and over the high Borrowdale Fells into Langdale. On and on they went and finally caught their fox at Coniston after darkness had set in, the pack not being gathered until the next day when the carcass was discovered. This was during Isaac Todhunter's term as Huntsman, which lasted from 1843-1869. The fur will 'slip' (fall out on touch) rather quickly on a dead fox, but if conditions were icy when this fox lay dead overnight at Coniston, then this would explain why the carcass had been preserved enough to be suitable for the taxidermist.

A very early photo of Willie Irving and his Melbreak hounds.

Notable Huntsmen of the Blencathra

The Blencathra has had several good Huntsmen at the helm, but some have become legends, even in their own lifetimes. Two of the most noteworthy were Jim Dalton and Johnny Richardson, both of whom were great houndsmen, but also very capable terrier breeders. Many were the top working terriers bred by these two stalwarts of the Blencathra. Dalton bred some of the foundation stock used to create the hardy and versatile pedigree Lakeland terrier.

Early Lakeland terrier breeder Peter Long's own terriers, for instance, were extensively used to create early bloodlines from the late nineteenth century on into the 1920s, and his stock was largely bred down from the Jim Dalton strain Lakeland terriers, back to his famous Turk (born c.1900–1910).

It is interesting to note that the current Huntsman, Barry

Todhunter is only the seventh Huntsman to hold office with the Blencathra pack since 1826. Joshua Fearon was the first to hunt these hounds under the Mastership of the old Squire. Isaac Todhunter held office from 1843 until 1869.

Johnny Richardson has probably been the most famous and popular Huntsman of the Blencathra and he was born and raised at Watendlath, close to the Borrowdale Valley. Even as a young child, he was a great walker of those harsh mountains, and Johnny would always walk to school over the fells and down into the Borrowdale Valley.

Many a time he got a good soaking whilst on his travels over the rough ground of this bleak area. His mother would regularly dry his clothes by the fire after school and Johnny grew up knowing what it was to suffer hardship. His family owned a farm, so shepherding was in his blood, and it was to shepherding that Johnny turned during the off-season of each summer. He had a passion for hunting and began whipping-in to George Bell at the Blencathra in 1946 as Johnny returned from the war. Before this time he had hunted regularly with the Blencathra and Melbreak Foxhounds and he knew Willie Irving very well indeed.

His war years were eventful to say the least and he escaped from German prisoner of war camps on at least two occasions, eventually living with Italian families who sheltered him. He had also spent quite a few months, including during winter, living among the Apennine Mountains and no doubt these experiences of harsh conditions helped him to thrive as Huntsman on the bleak crags.

The language barrier in Italy between him and those who took him into their homes proved no barrier at all for, as Johnny himself stated, 'they were farmers, just like myself.' Johnny was one of life's gentlemen and he could get on with anybody, rich or poor alike. He was an expert with hounds and terriers and his abilities to get about the fells and his unending stamina made him a legend. Most fell packs carry lines back to Richardson's breeding programme and the Pennine Foxhounds of Holmfirth carry several lines back to his famous pack. He died in his sleep during the late 1980s, after a long service of over forty years at the hunt. Barry Todhunter, his young protégé, took over.

The Ullswater Foxhounds

The Ullswater Foxhounds were formed during the 1880s when the Matterdale and Patterdale Hounds were amalgamated, both originally trencher-fed packs working to control predator numbers, with the bounties claimed to finance them. When bounty payments stopped, several of these small packs disbanded altogether, or were amalgamated to form just the one pack which became kennelled and formally-run, the Matterdale and Patterdale Hunts coming together to form the Ullswater.

The new, professionally-run Ullswater Foxhounds were able to provide a very effective means of predator control (many different species were hunted until well into the twentieth century) and a great way of enjoying a busy social life.

Out of the hunting grew social activities including balls, dinners and games nights. Joe Bowman was possibly the greatest Huntsman this pack has produced, though Joe Wear was also a superb houndsman and was very popular with farmers and followers.

Anthony Barker, who hunted hounds during the Second World War while Wear was away, also made a great houndsman and this stood him in good stead when he later hunted the Windermere Harriers with the valuable assistance of his daughters, Heather and Diane. John Harrison is the current Huntsman of the Ullswater pack.

Jim Dalton with the Blencathra under Skiddaw in the mid-1920s. George Bell (left) and Doug Paisley behind Dalton (to the left).

The Coniston Foxhounds

The Coniston Foxhounds were started in 1825 by Anthony Gaskarth of Coniston Hall and it seems they were originally a trencher-fed pack of harriers, who focussed on hunting the hare, that were kept on various farms in the Coniston area.

Legend has it that Gaskarth, a farmer and butcher, had some persistent bad payers and with one of these, after exhausting all other avenues in order to try to have his bill settled, he exercised his legal right to seize property up to the value of the debt and confiscated two hounds that were part of an existing trencher-fed pack. Gaskarth, along with other enthusiasts then formed what became the Coniston Foxhounds.

It seems they didn't settle in one kennel for any great period of time until 1881, when suitable kennels were built at Greenbank, on the hill above Ambleside, where they remain to this day. Prior to this they were sometimes trencher-fed, while at other times they were kennelled, one of the sites being at Sawrey, with another at Coniston. George and Anthony Chapman, father and son, are the Coniston's most famous Huntsmen and they became popular legends, even in their own day.

The Coniston pack, under both of these Huntsmen, also produced some wonderfully game and typey terriers. The first Lakeland terrier champion, Evergreen's Double, was bred out of a long line of Coniston Hunt terriers used, and possibly bred by, George Chapman, though I suspect Ernie Towers and Jim Fleming of Grasmere may also have played a part in the breeding of some of these earth dogs. Stockbeck Sam, the sire of Deepdale Holloa (Rock) of the Melbreak, was out of Ribston Pippin and this bitch was descended from Coniston Metz, a white terrier and the ancestor of George Chapman and Ernie Towers' strain of Lakelands, subsequently brought into Willie Irving's breeding programme and probably Jim Fleming's too.

Metz was of fox terrier origin and was possibly descended from the terriers of Bobby Troughton who hunted the Dallam Tower Otterhounds, also known as the Kendal and District Otterhounds. Alternatively, Metz may have been bred down from Rawdon Lee's fox terriers, as Lee certainly worked his strain in and around this area. Mike Nicholson hunted the Coniston for several seasons and he is the grandson of Anthony Chapman, so hunting has been in his blood for several former generations.

Eskdale and Ennerdale Foxhounds

The Eskdale and Ennerdale Foxhounds were originally two separate packs and the Eskdale were set up in 1857 by 'laal' Tommy Dobson. A pack already existed at Ennerdale and they were originally known as the Scawfell Hounds, hunted by Will

Ritson and later by his son, John, before control passed to the Nicholsons. But they struggled to keep going and so these two hunts amalgamated under the Mastership of Tommy Dobson, becoming a combined subscription pack in the 1880s in order to survive around the time that bounty payments were being stopped.

Several hunting songs were written to commemorate the life and times of Tommy Dobson and the following is just one of these, with the composer unknown:

Blencathra hound puppies – always popular with the children.

The fame of 'laal' Dobson has often been sung
As through those fine valleys his deep voice it rung
But he suddenly gave a last blast of his horn
In the sweet valley of Langdale, one dark Sunday morn.

The Omnipotent Being saw him 'git away'
Like a fox in the chase he had no time to stay
All means they were tried his life for to save
But he's gone now to rest in his dark earthly grave.

As a mark of respect for a warrior so brave
We will place a tombstone at the head of his grave
For the thousands of miles he has tramped oe'r the rocks
While hunting the otter, the badger and fox.

There ne'er was a hunter so honest and sound
As the late Tommy Dobson, that's gone to the ground.
To lose such a sportsman it seems very hard
But his body's now resting in Eskdale churchyard.

Dobson was as keen a hound and terrier man as could be found. His longest hunt was seventeen hours in duration, which was in pursuit of a lamb-killing fox during springtime (see *Willie Irving, Terrierman, Huntsman and Lakelander* by Sean Frain, published by Merlin Unwin Books). Several other hunts were noteworthy too, such as the one arranged after a Mr Dixon had lost several geese to a marauding fox.

The meet was at Birkby Fell during November in the late 1890s and the day was dull and grey, with endless streams of cloud above. Reynard was found out on the fells not far from the farm and he crossed wide moors and took in dense woodlands wherever possible, before heading down for the low country where he swam the river Esk, hoping to shake off his relentless pursuers.

Hounds kept at him, however, and pushed him among the lowland pastures and woodlands of Eskdale, so he now made for the higher places for security. He was so hard-pressed, though, despite his best efforts to thwart the hunt, that he sought refuge at Lingbeck Ghyll, making for an earth in the crags. Rose, a game Eskdale and Ennerdale terrier, was put in and it seems she worried the fox below, which was eventually dug out. This hunt put an end to the geese-worrying and had been of long duration, covering many miles of hard country.

Newspaper accounts from the 1920s and 30s indicate that a small pack was still kept in the Ennerdale area into the early twentieth century and it was said that Willie Irving had spent some time hunting with these as a lad, when Will Nicholson hunted this pack. Of course, these accounts may not be accurate,

Will Scott and the Dumfriesshire otterhounds.

though they were written from interviews with local hunting folk who lived at the time and had a great knowledge of hunting in the fells. Willie Porter took over from Tommy Dobson and he inherited the pack on Dobson's death in 1910. The Eskdale and Ennerdale Hounds remain in the Porter family to this day and Edmund, Willie Porter's grandson, continues to act as Master and Huntsman after over five decades of dedicated service.

The Lunesdale Foxhounds

The Lunesdale Foxhounds are kennelled a few miles from Sedbergh and they hunt in the Yorkshire Dales and parts of Cumbria. It seems they were originally kennelled in the Sedbergh area, but moved to Orton, near Tebay, probably when they were reformed. This pack, now hunted by Paul Whitehead, was originally founded and hunted by Tommy Robinson, possibly using hounds from the old Wensleydale Foxhounds that were disbanded in 1907, and were known as the Sedbergh and Lunesdale Foxhounds until they too were disbanded in 1927.

However, the packs were reformed in 1930 by Tommy Robinson, Harold Watson and Harold Hodgson. Walter Parkin became Whipper-in, eventually taking over as Huntsman and hunting hounds with great success until his retirement in 1963. John Nicholson took over from Parkin and he remained with the hunt for several years, hunting hounds with great expertise for the next three decades or so.

Maurice Bell, Master and Huntsman of the Wensleydale Foxhounds, relates fascinating tales of hunting with Walt Parkin on the wild fells of the Dales and Bell states that Parkin was a real expert with hounds, rarely interfering and allowing them to get on with their job, which often consisted of them following a cold drag for hours before a fox was eventually roused and hunting proper could begin.

Parkin was a fearless man who would stand right on the edge of sheer-drop crags to watch his hounds at work and a fell walker of renown, becoming one of the great Huntsmen of the fell hunting world. He was also a famous terrier breeder and the fact that Cyril Breay and Frank Buck infused their terrier strains with Parkin's dogs is testimony indeed to the abilities of his stock.

Lunesdale Huntsman John Nicholson, born and bred at Ambleside, learnt much of his trade from Anthony Chapman. Nicholson, who began whipping-in to Parkin in 1950, and later became Huntsman, was renowned for his fitness, and most days would see him out on the fells walking upwards of twenty miles.

Entire weeks were sometimes spent away from home, hunting outlying areas. Kennels were then at Orton near Tebay; the present Cautley site was only purchased during the 1960s. Nicholson took over in 1963 and he, like his predecessor, was a great fell walking man. Even at the age of 65 he could climb those fells quicker than most and, because of this, as because of his skills at turning out a fit and hard working pack of hounds, he became a legend in his own lifetime.

The Lake District has produced several of Britain's most noteworthy hunting figures: perhaps it is the landscape, or maybe the local genes of this rugged race, that shapes such individuals.

'Laal' Tommy Dobson, legendary Master of the Eskdale & Ennerdale foxhounds.

3

THE STRUCTURE OF A FELL PACK

From the early 19th century, all of the fell packs were formed through the amalgamation of much smaller packs that were originally trencher-fed and kept mostly by farmers and miners, though a good number of quarrymen also kept hounds and a brace or two of terriers.

The old system in which vermin bounties could be claimed meant the economic survival of packs even during times of industrial hardship (of which the Lake District has had more than its fair share!).

It was the setting up of committees and the formation of subscription packs that meant hunting could become far more organised and a useful form of social activity too. Committees raised funds for the pack and provided good kennelling, via hunt balls, country shows and other activities.

These activities meant that enough funds could be raised to feed hounds, maintain kennels and pay hunt staff. Although run by committees, some hunts remained privately owned and this has been the case of the Eskdale and Ennerdale pack. Although the Porter family have owned the hounds since the death of Tommy Dobson, the Huntsman and Whipper-in have always been paid by the Committee and the kennels have been purchased and maintained by them too.

The old system of using a trencher-fed pack, with hounds being brought together on hunting days only, was obviously cheaper, but this system is not as effective. Trencher-fed hounds do not work as well together as those that spend much time in kennels, neither do they respond as well to their Huntsman. Hounds must form a close bond with their Huntsman if they are to work well for him and a trencher-fed pack does not get the opportunity to do this. Also, discipline and control is easier with a kennelled pack, in relation to livestock and sheep-worrying. So it is far better to have them in kennel and to hunt them under the present system.

Economics of running a pack

Keeping a pack of hounds in kennel is rather an expensive business and so a unique system was adopted in the fell country that saw hounds come together for the hunting season only. After hunting finished, hounds were split up again and they returned to farms and village cottages where they had been walked as puppies.

The Huntsman and Whipper-in were paid a small retainer fee and then released from duties in order to find work that would keep themselves and their families for the summer months, until hunting resumed again in September and the hunt staff took up their duties once more. And so a skeleton trencher-fed system remained in place, outside the hunting season. This afforded hounds the time to rest and recuperate after a very hard and taxing few months hunting out on open fell, though not all hounds had what one would call 'a rest period'.

And this trencher-fed method had other advantages. At one time several otter hunting packs existed in the Lake District and most of these were formed using hounds 'out at walk' during the summer from the local fell packs. Otters were once very numerous in Cumbria and so great days were enjoyed along rivers, becks and around lakes, meres and tarns.

Many of the terriers that served with foxhounds during the winter were also in action at otter during the summer. These terriers were often called upon all year round to work a variety of quarry. Notebooks left by the late Willie Irving record that he sent some of his terriers to serve at Otterhound kennels during the summer months when his beloved Melbreak pack were temporarily disbanded out of fox-hunting season, and most other Huntsmen did likewise.

This semi-trencher-fed system has worked so well that it is still in use today and helps keep the running costs of a hunt down to some extent, though it has a far more useful purpose than just this. Having hounds walked with local farmers and villagers is a great way to keep the pack well-socialised, which also cuts down on the risk of several potential problems including sheep-worrying, fighting with other dogs or killing cats.

In summary, under the semi-trencher-fed system, hounds grow up in regular contact with children, other dog breeds, cats

Johnny Richardson leads his Blencathra pack at Bassenthwaite.

and farm livestock, learning to leave well alone. They are well-adjusted by the time they begin hunting and are let loose on the fells and around farms and villages where hunts often take them. A well-behaved hound is essential and those that take to killing livestock are usually put down immediately, which stops the problem from spreading to other pack members and ensures good control in the future.

Some hounds do take to worrying livestock, especially sheep which run from hounds in a blind panic, seemingly inviting them to give chase. Willie Irving recorded that he put down a few hounds over the years, usually for sheep worrying and in 1937 he wrote that Matchless and Crystal were put down, though he failed to state why, while Dimple was killed and Magic died of distemper.

During the 1928/29 season Melbreak Badger worried a sheep at Newlands and was destroyed, with Manuel and Marksman also being put down, possibly for the same reason. Lilac was another Melbreak hound destroyed that season and Comely died, probably at work. Some hounds were put down because they wouldn't work, so one cannot assume that every hound destroyed was a sheep-worrier.

Job of the committees

The committees saw to it that funds were raised to kennel and keep hounds and they also appointed the Huntsman and Whipper-in who were both usually local people, though sometimes outsiders did manage to obtain posts. Welshman Maldwin Williams, for instance, became Whipper-in at the Ullswater Foxhounds under the Huntsmanship of Joe Wear, and Williams became a hard fell walker who proved to be a great asset to the hunt. In fact, he was offered the job of Huntsman when Wear retired, but turned down the opportunity and returned to Wales, his native land.

Otterhounds in early spring.

Christopher Ogilvie became Whipper-in, then Huntsman, to the Coniston Foxhounds and he too was not a native of Cumbria, though he spent quite a lot of time in the Lakes and had much hunt service experience before this time.

Hunt committees organised hunt balls, whist drives, games nights, coffee mornings, hound, stick and terrier shows, as well as sheepdog trials, in order to raise money for hunt funds, and there was at one time even a beauty contest run by some of the fell packs.

Many of these activities continue today and auctions are also held in order to help raise money. Also, money is left to hunts on the deaths of some of the wealthier followers and this goes a long way to ensuring a secure future for the pack involved. Others donate large amounts of money on occasion and this too helps secure the future of fell hunting.

However, in the early days, before committees took the helm and most packs were privately owned, subscriptions were sometimes obtained and funds were raised at hunt socials, usually held at the Inn were a meet had taken place that day.

Willie Porter sets off with the Eskdale & Ennerdale pack from the Angler's Inn (now demolished). The date is about 1900.

Potato pie was the main staple and good quantities of ale were enjoyed, while monies were paid to the innkeeper and all profits donated to the running costs of the hunt. Kennels, if it was not a trencher-fed pack, were usually very small outbuildings and so maintenance was cheap enough, with some kennels being built free of charge.

Materials and labour were often provided at no cost and farmers provided fallen stock for feed, so running costs were low indeed. However, some funds were necessary, for medical treatment and for compensating those who had sheep killed by a rogue hound.

The Huntsman's job is not an easy one. Most Huntsmen were from farming stock and so to wish to account for a predator which had taken a heavy toll of livestock such as geese, chickens and lambs, has been a traditional instinct found in each successive generation of Huntsmen. There have been some poor ones, but the vast majority of Huntsmen have been experts at their trade. A Huntsman who experiences a dry spell of no finds, or poor hunts, might find his reputation on the line, but such dry spells, if his hound-breeding policies and kennel husbandry were sound, would not last for long.

It was the Huntsman's job to first find a fox and this he did by loosing his pack, usually after a meet at a local inn, in the low country and then heading out onto the fells to draw likely places. He would tend to take the same route, more or less, in that area, and hounds would spread, or fan, out and search with their nostrils constantly seeking out any lingering scent, no matter how faint.

When a fox was found, the Huntsman would then cheer on his pack in an attempt to get them together as quickly as possible. More often than not they would follow a drag for an hour or more, even for half the day in John Peel's time when fell hunting was conducted at a slower pace than in more modern times, until the fox was eventually found and afoot.

Hounds would then 'speak' eagerly to a fresh line and all would get together and hunt Charlie for two, three, four, or more hours. Some hunts lasted for even eight hours, with one of the longest being twelve hours, when Willie Irving was Huntsman of the Melbreak.

A role of the early Huntsman had been to use 'tufters' to find the their prey, initially deer. This was later adapted to become a system of fox hunting unique to the Lake District. The

Huntsman would put a few hounds into cover to flush their prey and various followers stationed themselves in likely locations, along with a couple of waiting hounds; very often the ones they had 'walked' for the hunt. When Reynard was finally found, the coupled hounds were loosed and joined the others in following the line. The main aim was to catch the fox. Remember, in the fells, control of foxes had been the main aim of hunters, not sport. And so this method worked well but gradually fell into disuse towards Peel's time.

With the current ban on hunting with packs, could we see a return to similar methods? Only time will tell, but putting a couple of hounds into covert in order to flush to waiting guns remains legal, while coupled hounds could be in various places with selected followers and these could be loosed only in order to continue flushing a fox towards guns. This would be a legal way of keeping hounds working in the fells, though shooting foxes in such areas is incredibly risky, with ramblers and walkers scattered in almost every part of the Lakes country. Guns would of necessity have to 'hold hard' and only shoot foxes when clean, clear and safe shots presented themselves.

Once hounds were on the line of their fox, the Huntsman could merely try to keep in touch with his pack, urge them on or lift their spirits if they were struggling, and maybe help out at a check or hindrance if he managed to catch up with them. Sometimes a Huntsman could get in front of his pack and stop them if they were about to cross a wide river with no bridges nearby that would allow followers to travel in their wake, but being able to accomplish this was rare indeed.

A fell pack fairly flew when hunting a fox and just keeping them in view was difficult enough. This problem has resulted in road casualties and crag-fast hounds over the years. And these days, since the hunting act of 2004 (which came into effect in February 2005), it has had a bearing on hunting in the Lake

District: now hounds are only permitted to be at exercise, or hunting trail (artificial scent), as we shall see later.

At the end of a hunting day, the Huntsman would make sure that all his hounds were safely on hand and this he would do by 'blowing the gather'. Hounds can hear the sound of a horn for miles around and they will readily return, provided they can do so, and scent isn't strong. If scent is good, then hounds would run after dark and some hunts have ended late at night.

One of Irving's ended with a fox being run to ground at 11pm and then terrier work began! If any hounds failed to turn up, then it would be the job of the Huntsman to take his pack back to kennels, or to temporary accommodation if they were staying in an allocated area for the week.

There he would feed and bed down his pack and then search for missing hounds if daylight allowed. If not, he would look for them the following day, blowing his horn at regular intervals. Often though, hounds made their way back on their own, or went to the farm, or cottage, where they were originally walked. The next morning they would be loosed from their

The Blencathra foxhounds on top of a snowy Helvellyn in 1931.

walks and off they would trot, making their way back to kennels
by themselves

Gathering hounds

In modern times mechanised transportation has meant that
gathering and looking for hounds is much easier, though dangers
on busy roads have increased. Several hounds have been killed
on the roads whilst actually hunting foxes, or whilst making
their way home at the end of the day, sometimes during the
hours of darkness.

Personal anecdote – death on road of hounds

My wife and I found a Coniston hound that had been run over
when they were hunting the Cartmel Fell area. The meet, if I
remember correctly, had been at Bryan Beck and hounds had
soon found a fox in this populated area. Several were afoot, in
fact, but they were that year's youngsters and they stuck mainly
to dense woodland and undergrowth which, in October, hadn't
started to thin out.

Stan Mattinson, the Huntsman at that time, eventually
moved hounds on and they quickly had an adult fox on the run,
which gave a fast hunt all over the rolling hills of this area and
finally took them over the tops and dropped down through deep
woodlands all the way to the shores of Windermere.

The trouble was that Reynard crossed the busy lake road at
a time when hounds were pressing him very hard and unfortunately one of Stan's best bitches was knocked down and killed
instantly. We flagged down a car follower and her body was
taken back to kennels.

It was a sad loss and marred what had been a grand hunt.
Reynard re-crossed the road lower down, after skirting the

shores of Windermere, and made back into the woods, then back to the high country, where he evaded capture.

All of the fell packs can tell similar stories and even in the 1920s and 1930s some hounds were killed on roads, though back then this was a very rare occurrence and there was more of a chance of hounds killing a fox on a main road, than hounds being killed on one. This was the outcome of a hunt that featured the Coniston pack and, though I do not know the exact date, it seems it was during the 1930s when Ernie Parker was hunting them.

The Coniston Foxhounds were in the Rydal/Grasmere area and a fox was soon roused in Rydal Park, where the famous hound show is held each year. A 45 minute hunt followed that took in Scandale Fell and Hart Crag, and it was Black Crag that saw the demise of this gallant fox, with hounds rolling him over in fine style.

A second was afoot almost immediately and he climbed Fairfield towards Grisedale Pike. It seemed he was intent on reaching the heights of lofty Helvellyn, but he turned and made

Johnny Richardson (right) with 'Pritch' Bland pausing before they gather the Blencathra hounds above a rocky crag.

Otterhounds and foot-followers at St John's in the Vale.

back to his own country in a hurry. He passed by Great Rigg,
Stone Arthur and Forest Side, then got into Nab Scar as hounds
pressed him severely.

Here he tried all kinds of cunning tricks to throw them, but
scent was good and they stuck to their task until, at last, Reynard
was forced to make out of the scar.

Hounds hunted him relentlessly now and so Charlie fairly
flew, but could do nothing to shake them and so he was at last
accounted for on the main road near White Moss.

Cars were obviously far less of a threat back in those days and
hunting could continue without too much fear of hounds falling
to motorised transport. Such were the glory days of fell hunting
and often long, unhindered hunts were enjoyed.

The Eskdale and Ennerdale pack experienced some superb hunts during those glorious times when Willie Porter was in charge and one of his best was after the pack had returned from visiting the Ingleborough district for a few days of hunting in the Yorkshire Dales, where they had enjoyed quite a bit of success.

A fox was roused at Lingbeck Ghyll and he took them across Brantrake Fell and Moss, all the way to the tarn at Devoke, where some great fishing could be had in those days. Hounds flew on the line. Porter could only keep in touch by asking local shepherds which way they had run and one such shepherd informed Willie that hounds had killed at White Pike.

A second fox was found at Stainton Pike and he was pushed hard by the determined pack. Driven to Broad Oak, where 'laal' Tommy Dobson once lived before he settled at Eskdale, the fox swam the reservoir there and hounds followed, catching and killing him in the water after a splendid run. Followers were present at the finish and stated that it had been like watching an otter hunt, with hounds all swimming in the wake of their quarry.

Another cracking hunt was with Willie Irving and his Melbreak pack. Hounds met at Rogerscale and all were shown great hospitality by Colonel and Mrs Highet, who were keen followers during Irving's time as Huntsman. Willie loosed his hounds above the hamlet and they drew a lot of ground until they finally found on Dodd, with a fast hunt following.

Reynard took hounds across the vale, up mist-covered Fellbarrow and over Low Fell, with the hounds eventually coming out of the mist above Foulsyke. Only the grand music of the pack had kept followers in touch until now, but at last they were in view and a spectacular hunt was seen by all and sundry. Reynard now dropped down from the high country and crossed the Loweswater/Lamplugh road, making through swampy ground and eventually across to Melbreak, where several fresh foxes saved his life as they ran out from Mowdy Crags and led the hounds away from their original 'pilot'.

A grand hunt ensued that saw hounds having much difficulty among the boulder-strewn mountainside, but they picked up the pace about Pillar Rake and one of the foxes made to earth near the top of the Saddle. Willie put in a brace of terriers and a dog fox soon bolted, which was quickly accounted for by hounds. A second fox proved to be to ground and was worried below by the terriers. Some wonderful hunting was enjoyed in those days before Huntsmen had to worry too much about busy roads.

The Huntsman would cover several miles during any hunting day, averaging between fifteen and twenty miles, with outstanding days seeing them walk over thirty miles. In the old days they would have to walk back to kennels, or lodgings, after hunting and then begin checking over the pack for injuries and feeding and bedding them down for the night.

Injuries would be treated promptly and all of this was done before hunt staff saw to themselves. Paws would have to be checked, as rocks could split pads and this made hounds lame for some time afterwards, especially if the wound wasn't thoroughly cleaned and treated as soon as possible. Good food and dry, warm kennels helped keep a pack in good shape and if well-kept, they would serve their Huntsman well.

Different methods of caring for hounds

Several Huntsmen were noted for keeping their hounds in fine fettle and Willie Irving, Walter Parkin and Joe Wear were foremost among these Huntsmen. Eddie Pool says that Wear would spend an age after hunting, carefully checking each hound for thorns in the flesh and cuts to their pads, then he would treat any with injuries before seeing to his own comforts. It was important to be thorough in this regard, in order to avoid infections taking hold and becoming deep-rooted; usually the result of untreated injuries. This took time and patience after a hard day's hunting, but the rewards were well worth the effort, especially during those times when antibiotics and penicillin were not available.

A cut pad soaked in salt water two or three times a day would help keep the wound clean and infection-free and this would also aid quick healing. Eyes would be checked too and any debris left from drawing through undergrowth and woodland would immediately be removed and the eye cleaned. Terriers were seen to in a similar manner and fox bites would be promptly treated. Bits of soil and grit could be a problem in the eyes of terriers used to ground and such were carefully checked and cleaned at the end of each working day. A hunting day, as we have seen, was a busy time for any Huntsman.

A Huntsman would also have to keep the kennels in good condition, cleaning and disinfecting them on a regular basis. Diseases such as distemper did strike at times, but such infections could often be kept at bay by good kennel management. Isolating the infected hound and regularly scrubbing the kennels would help prevent the spread of the disease. Pregnant and nursing bitches were given extra care and attention and this could keep a Huntsman busy, even out of season, though some followers did assist with raising puppies.

The Huntsman would also be responsible for the rescue of crag-fast hounds and terriers trapped to ground, although much assistance was available from regular hunt followers who were always keen to lend a hand at such times. Still, the duties were many and varied and a Huntsman was fortunate if he had the assistance of a full-time Whipper-in.

During the summertime, the Huntsman had to find other paid employment, but there would still be plenty to do around the kennels in looking after any hounds and terriers not 'out at walk' ie not back with their original 'carers'. Hounds and terriers being exhibited need careful preparation, taking time and effort.

The Whipper-in

The Whipper-in must of necessity be a keen houndsman. He may walk a hound or two, maybe even a brace of terriers, during the off-season, although the Whipper-in didn't generally assist the Huntsman off-season, but sought employment elsewhere for the summer, leaving the Huntsman to care for any hounds left in kennel. A Whipper-in's duty included helping to prepare food and feed hounds, as well as cleaning out the kennel buildings,

The Bucks otterhounds visit Hexham Bridge in 1951 (see Chapter 9, page 179).

and assisting in treating any wounds found on hounds or terriers at the end of the hunting day.

But it was during hunting itself that the Whipper-in was most useful. Whilst the Huntsman drew through fellsides or dense woodlands, the Whipper-in would climb out onto the fell-tops and keep a close look out which way Reynard went. Being out on the tops, he was often in a better position to keep with the hounds, provided he had chosen the right spot in which to stand once the fox had been roused, with the Huntsman catching up later as best he could.

A Whipper-in would need to be just as fit as the man in charge and he too would cover endless miles in the wake of the pack. Sometimes a Whip needed to be fitter, as he could be sent back to kennels to fetch a terrier that was narrow enough to get into an earth where others were struggling.

When a terrier didn't emerge, the Whipper-in was often left at the earth to await its re-emergence or to dig it out if needed, though some of the keener Huntsmen who loved terrier work too, such as Willie Irving and Jim Dalton, would often be found digging to their terrier themselves, even after having taken hounds home and seen to their needs first.

Famous Lake District Whippers-in

There have been some famous Whippers-in among the various fell packs and Maldwin Williams was one of the best. 'Pritch' Bland, the late Melbreak Huntsman, spoke very highly of Williams, as did others, saying that he could walk all day at a rather fast pace and then dig up half a fellside in order to reach terrier and fox. Braithwaite Wilson, who later hunted the Ullswater Foxhounds for a few seasons after Joe Bowman retired, was known as 'the flying Whip' by Ullswater followers as he set a fast pace across those bleak mountains. Bill Braithwaite was another hard-walking Whipper-in of more recent times, who assisted Maurice Bell at the Wensleydale Foxhounds. Some Whips never go on to become Huntsmen and this is usually because they get married, start families and just cannot afford to live off such low wages. Some, however, stick at it and eventually take over when the Huntsman retires.

Few of the fell packs today, if any, have a Whipper-in, though there are always keen followers who will assist with hunting hounds.

Car followers also play a vital role, not only in giving financial assistance, but also in providing a great service when hounds approach roads. They will then either stop hounds, or stop traffic, thus allowing hounds to cross safely. It is a shame that the traditional Whipper-in is now not found in the fell packs, but finances dictate that hunts must keep costs to a minimum. Hunting hounds is a very expensive business these days, so Huntsmen are usually single-handed in the kennels, though amateur Whips do assist on hunting days.

On a hunting day, the Whipper-in would take a different route to the Huntsman, though generally speaking these two hunt servants wouldn't be too far apart and they would often join up during the course of an average day.

When they met up, the Huntsman would give instructions to his Whip if, for example, hounds split, or someone was needed to remain at an earth, or to fetch a terrier from kennels, or from a nearby farm, though in more recent times CB radios have provided a great means of keeping in touch, not only with the Whipper-in but between foot and car followers too and this has meant that it is much easier to follow hounds. If foot followers didn't know which way hounds had gone, then car followers usually did.

Modern technology has meant that hunting in the fells has become easier and cars and CBs have saved much legwork for both followers and hunt staff alike. Nowadays hounds can be taken by vehicle to the meet and be picked up again at the finish of hunting for that day.

In earlier times, even up to the 1960s, hounds walked to the meet from either kennels or lodgings, then returned on foot again after a hard day out on the fells. It was a hard existence for all concerned. Hunting a pack of fellhounds today remains far from easy, despite labour-saving devices, but it was much harder before the car.

Dalesman (C. N. de Courcy Parry) whipped-in to the famous Joe Bowman in those times when fell hunting was at its hardest, tramping to meets and back to kennels at the close of the day. Dalesman later went on to hunt his own hounds, though he also followed several other packs, some mounted, some on foot.

He wrote a number of books and articles, including *Foxhunting for Children and Other Simple Tales*, an illustration from which I have included in this book (see overleaf). Copies of this old book are rare these days, though I recently saw something in *Hounds* magazine about it being reprinted, but under a different title. Dalesman was an ardent hunter who covered miles of fell country with his hounds.

Lodging hounds

Until the 1970s, and occasionally still today, a system of lodging hounds for a week at various inns and farms throughout a hunt country was widely introduced, while a more remote area was hunted, although this practise had been in existence for a number of centuries, particularly in Scotland where professional pest controllers travelled long distances in search of work and stayed at any dwelling hospitable enough to provide shelter.

No doubt barns and other farm outbuildings played host to these 'Todhunters', though a few nights were probably spent under the stars too.

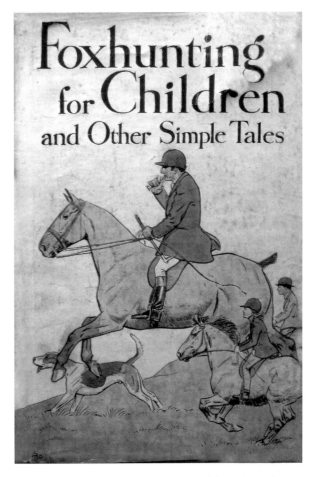

The cover of Dalesman's book for children about hunting.

In the Lake District the farmers and innkeepers, many of whom were related, began playing host to the pack visiting their area and there was often a hunt ball held during that week of hunting when as many foxes as possible would be accounted for. This generated funds and helped keep folk interested in fell hunting, keeping youngsters involved, thus ensuring the future existence of these packs. Hounds very often visited local schools before hunting began and the children enjoyed stroking hounds and terriers, which have traditionally displayed great temperaments. Food was put on when the hunt visited and the famous 'tattie pot' reigned supreme as the chosen dish with which to feed 'hunters all'. This was a kind of stew, mainly made up of mutton and potatoes.

Legend states that John Peel would go on three or four day drinking sessions after a good hunt, not being seen again until he felt he had had enough celebrating and returned home. Willie Porter was said to head off on a Monday and not be seen again till Thursday, or even later, if scenting was good. This doesn't mean that Willie hunted for days on end: it simply shows that he travelled around and stayed in different areas whilst hunting them. It seems John Peel had a similar arrangement and stayed at various Lake District farms and inns.

This would explain his so-called three-day drinking sprees after he had killed a fox. Rather than drinking at the inn for three days, he was simply staying there for a week of hunting in a far-flung area of his hunt country (Peel hunted as far north as the Scottish Borders), though I have no doubt that he did enjoy a celebration after hunting. Tales are told of his horses taking him home along the pitch-black country lanes after a night out at one of the inns within reach of his home, the sleeping Huntsman draped over the horse's back, snoring loudly as he traversed the dark countryside.

4

D'YE KEN JOHN PEEL?

One of the Lake District's most famous sons, John Peel (1777-1854), became a worldwide icon. His father William Peel, a dealer in horseflesh, particularly the fell ponies which can still be found in Cumbria today, married Lettice Scott at Caldbeck church in 1776. In 1777 they had a son whom they named John. He was the first of thirteen children and they lived at Park End, Caldbeck, when John was born. The Peel family were farming stock through and through and John's grandfather was a well-known chicken and pig farmer, known as 'Cock and Bacon' Peel, who farmed at Ireby.

They were not rich, but William Peel kept his head above water by farming and general dealing, with John soon following in his father's footsteps. John was particularly fond of fell ponies and rode them from an early age. Making a living was extremely tough in the Lake District so many families took to a spot of poaching in order to survive. No doubt the young John Peel engaged in trout and salmon fishing, as well as rabbit-catching with ferrets and nets, and possibly snares too. He may also have found seasonal work at other farms in the area and he probably learnt how to plough as a boy too.

It seems he was an exceptional rider even as a lad and would ride bareback on any horse he came across, no matter to whom it belonged. He was undoubtedly a bit of a rogue and an

John Peel, as depicted by John Woodcock Graves.

independent lad from his early years. Such qualities would stand him in good stead later.

The Peel family was noted for longevity. Young John grew into a strong boy, the fields and moors of his area full of rabbits and the many becks and rivers teemed with fish, as they do today, so there would be no shortage of good, fresh food, provided young Peel could keep one step ahead of local gamekeepers! Clothing was made locally, in Caldbeck itself, a tough, hand-woven tweed made at a mill still to be seen in this charming village today. His footwear was traditional wooden clogs, again made in Caldbeck, which were very tough and durable, ideal for the fell country.

Mining for lead and copper was also carried out in this part of Cumbria, but there is no evidence that Peel ever worked in this industry. Like his father and grandfather before him, he stuck to farming for a living.

Drag hunting Lake District style

Even as a young lad he followed hounds with great eagerness and he hunted with any pack within reach, whether for deer, hare, fox, otter, pinemarten or polecat; it was all the same to him. He had a fondness for hounds working out a line and he would go on to have one of the finest drag-hunting packs in the north, even the whole country.

Drag-hunting in Cumbria was unique in that it did not involve, as is generally understood, following artificial scent for sport, but the stale scent of a live fox that had passed through the countryside several hours before hounds were cast off. In the Lake District, it is often the case that a fox will drop down into the low country overnight, to catch its prey, then just before first light it will return to the high fells. In the morning, the Hunt could meet in the low country for the pleasure of watching the hounds following the fox's scent (his cold drag) for several hours before tracking it to the high fells where they would eventually get first sight of the fox and the hunt proper could begin. Peel's hounds in particular were noted for sticking to a drag, often for several hours at a time, before at last finding their quarry.

It seems the method of 'tufting' (having a few hounds draw covert, ie search a wood in order to find quarry) wasn't carried out in the area Peel hunted, probably because the area is so bleak and open. It seems 'tufters' were used in areas of dense coverts, such as in the south of Cumbria, where large tracts of woodland provided great hiding places for foxes.

Peel engaged in cockfighting, like his grandfather before him, who probably bred gamecocks, but this 'sport' was different in the Lake District to the rest of the UK. Gamecocks were treasured by Cumbrian farmers and villagers and fights were

George Bell, the Blencathra Huntsman, with the whip Johnny Richardson (left) in the 1940s.

not to the death. No artificial spurs were used and death, even serious injury, was avoided. Cocks were needed to keep hens laying fertile eggs and owners didn't want them being killed or even injured, so fights were only until one cockerel clearly dominated another and then they were stopped. Such activities are now rightly illegal, but Cumbrian cockfighting was far more humane than cockfighting elsewhere in which the loser, sometimes even both combatants, were disembowelled before dying. Peel also enjoyed watching, and no doubt participating in, Cumberland and Westmorland wrestling. He was a big, strong lad and no doubt made a formidable opponent for anyone who took him on.

Young John Peel eventually turned his eye to the bonny Cumbrian lasses and he met a local girl by the name of Mary White whose parents farmed at Uldale. However, Peel was nearing his twenties and may well have had a reputation as a bit of a wild lad, for Mary's parents objected to the courtship and flatly refused to allow their daughter to marry him. It seems that, even in the wilds of far-flung Cumberland, parents wished their daughters to marry sensibly.

Peel may already have been spending much time with hounds and it seems he was fond of a celebration after hunting too, when he should have been working, and this is probably another reason why the Whites were so against their daughter marrying him. However, John Peel wasn't deterred and he persuaded Mary to run away with him to Gretna Green.

In the dead of night he made his way through the pitch-black country lanes on one of his father's best horses and picked up Mary, who had sneaked out of the house as quietly as possible, and off they rode, crossing the border into Scotland later that day, where they were married over the blacksmith's anvil. Perhaps William Peel had a hand in this arrangement and had encouraged his son in this endeavour, as he and his wife had eloped in

Joe Wear with his Ullswater hounds.

just the same way and had also been married at Gretna Green in the 1770s.

The rebellious pair now had to face the wrath of Mary's parents, but, although they were upset, they relented, realising their daughter was in love and that it was now futile to stand their ground against the arrangement. Instead of making more of a fuss, they asked that the pair marry 'properly' and they happily obliged. The ceremony was at Caldbeck church on 18 December 1797. John and Mary Peel went on to have thirteen children and they started life at Park End with Peel's parents.

They eventually moved to Upton in 1803, which is where Peel first began keeping his own hounds, though he had already hunted a great deal and may well have kept a hound or two for some local trencher-fed pack.

Peel was never a well-off man and he struggled to keep his pack throughout his life, but no doubt the bounty system helped during those early years when he could claim for the tails, or heads, of any predators his hounds caught. Peel and his family lived at Upton until about 1823 when they moved to Ruthwaite at Ireby, where Peel died in 1854.

Like his father, John Peel made a living from general farming and horse dealing and this brought him into contact with sporting farmers far and near. He knew a lot of folk in the borders of Scotland and he was later invited to hunt some of these border districts. It was while staying at local inns, or remote farms, that Peel's reputation for carousing began to grow. Locals would see Peel head off to a distant hunting ground and he wouldn't return for three or four days at a time.

After his death this reputation grew until Peel became known as one who couldn't stop drinking after he had killed a fox. What rubbish! True, Peel was at times a heavy drinker, we know that from eyewitness accounts, but the same could be said of many folk at the time or even today.

Heavy drinking is nothing unusual and several fell pack Huntsmen have been known to drink freely after hunting, or at summer shows. Peel was not unique in this regard, but that is not to say he went on two and three day drinking sprees. He would no doubt enjoy drinking each evening he was away staying at inns and farms, but hunting was his main focus, so much so that his farm somewhat was neglected, though his sons and daughters, as they grew, no doubt helped greatly around the place whilst he was away.

Peel hunted in a grey coat made from wool known as Hodden, or Skiddaw, Grey, woven locally at Caldbeck. Some stated that Peel wore a red coat, but that is incorrect, as John Woodcock-Graves, the composer of the famous song *D'ye Ken John Peel?* and one who knew Peel personally, unequivocally stated that it was grey and hand-woven at the Caldbeck mill.

Wilfred Lawson MP, the one-time Master of the Cumberland Hunt, hunted with Peel in his younger days, leaving a fascinating account of the old Huntsman, which is as follows:

'I have seen John Peel in the flesh and have hunted with him. He was a tall, bony Cumbrian who, when I knew him, used to ride a pony called Dunny, from its light colour, and on this animal, from his intimate knowledge of the country, he used to get along the roads and see a great deal of what his hounds did. Peel's gray coat is no more a myth than himself, for I well remember the long, rough, gray garment which almost came down to his knees.

No doubt drink played a prominent part – if it were not, indeed, the 'predominant partner' in these northern hunts. I have heard Peel say, when they had killed a fox, "Now! This is the first fox we've killed this season an' it be a dry 'un!" Words of that kind being a prelude to an adjournment to the nearest public house,

Willie Porter with his Eskdale & Ennerdale foxhounds in the 1930s. Douglas Paisley is far left.

where the party would remain for an indefinite time, reaching
– I have heard it said – even to two days.'

Notice that Lawson stated that he had 'heard it said' that
Peel went on two-day drinking sprees after a hunt, and that
he hadn't actually witnessed such events, although he hunted
regularly with Peel. Peel undoubtedly celebrated his hunting in
those days, but packs all over the country hunted into the early
afternoon and then headed off to an inn, or country house, for
celebrations. Peel was wild and did drink too heavily on these
occasions, often having to be put on his horse afterwards, which
would then take him home of its own accord. Notice too in
Lawson's account that the coat was grey – so the song should
read 'grey', and not 'gay' (which is how some versions render
this word). Incidentally, the word 'grey' was written as 'gray' in
pre-Victorian and 'gray' became another nickname for a badger,
because of its grey colouring.

It was during the latter half of the nineteenth century that
Thomas McMechan of Wigton, who was the Editor of *The
Wigton Advertiser*, wrote to John Woodcock-Graves, who had by
then emigrated to Tasmania, enquiring as to the origins of the
song. His reply was fascinating and went, in part, as follows:

'Nearly forty years have passed since John Peel and I sat in a snug
parlour at Caldbeck.

'We were then in the heyday of manhood and hunters of
the older fashion; meeting the night before to arrange earth
stopping and in the morning to take the best part of the hunt
– the drag over the mountains in the mist – while fashionable
hunters still lay in their blankets. Large flakes of snow fell that
evening. We sat by the fireside hunting over again many a good
run and recalling the feats of each particular hound, or narrow
neck-break 'scapes, when a flaxen-haired daughter of mine came
in the room, saying; "Father, what do they say to what granny

sings?" Granny was singing to sleep my eldest son (now a leading barrister in Hobart Town) with a very old rant called *Bonnie (or Cannie) Annie.* The pen and ink for hunting appointments being on the table, the idea of writing a song to this old air forced itself upon me and thus was produced, impromptu;

'Did ye ken John Peel wid his cwote sae gray?
Did ye ken John Peel at the breck 'o the day
Did ye ken John Peel gayin' far, far away
Wie his hoons and his horn in a mwornin'?'

Immediately after I sung it to poor Peel, who smiled through a stream of tears which fell down his manly cheeks, I well remember saying to him in a joking style, "By Jove, Peel, You'll be sung when we're both run to earth."'

Joe Bowman's funeral in the Spring of 1940. The Mardale meets (see page 91) were never the same without 'Old Joe'.

Graves mentions arranging earth stopping, which tells us that Peel had a terrierman. Earth stopping could only be practised in the low country, because stopping borrans and crag earths on fellsides is impossible, though badger setts found on the fells may well have been stopped when Peel was in the area (badger setts were few and far between as terriermen and gamekeepers eagerly dug them out).

The terriers would be a rough and ready lot, varied in type, though the Lowther Castle strain of fell terriers would undoubtedly have played a part, as such dogs could be found on almost every farm and in every village in the northern fells. These were simply known as coloured working terriers. Peel seems to have had very little interest in terriers, although he probably kept a number himself throughout his lifetime and may well have run them with hounds, which was common practise in those days.

John Peel as a Huntsman has received criticism for neglecting both his farm and his family. Huntsmen everywhere, but more so in the fells, where staying away from home for several days

Walt Parkin at the Melmerby Meet in the early 1950s.

at a time was often essential, meant that much time was indeed spent away from the family circle. Peel had a farm to run, as well as a family to raise, but as his sons and daughters grew older they could cope while their father was away hunting different areas. Peel lived in an age when predators were hunted down ruthlessly and farmers far and wide called on Peel to hunt their land and keep foxes at bay. These farmers could not be neglected if good land was to be kept by a pack.

Peel was passionate about hound work and loved to hunt, but he was also a farmer and kept his establishment going against great odds for fifty years or more, whilst having to cover vast distances with his small pack of hounds.

On one occasion, Peel was called out at the worst time possible, after his son, Peter, had died at the age of 27 and his funeral was about to take place. A local farmer had been losing geese to a marauding fox and Peel was asked to deal with the problem. At dawn on the day of his son's funeral in 1840, Peel was out with his hounds and they hit off a drag close to the farm where geese had been taken. Peel encouraged his hounds on as they followed the drag until, at last, they had their fox away. Peel hunted down this thieving beast and killed it later in the day.

However, he made it back in time for his son's burial and threw the fox carcass onto the coffin. Peel has been greatly criticised for going hunting on that day. But death in Georgian Britain was part of everyday living and folk had to get on with their lives. It was Peel's duty, to answer the calls of local farmers having trouble with predators and to deal with them promptly.

So Peel had no choice but to answer the call and bringing home the carcass of the problem fox to put across the coffin was his tribute to his son. This act may also indicate that Peter Peel had shown interest in hunting and that his father was proud that he was following in his footsteps, until his life was tragically cut short.

Peel had only a modest income so keeping hounds on a large scale was out of the question. His pack became part kennelled, part trencher-fed. He couldn't afford to keep many hounds in kennel at his farm at Upton and, later, at Ruthwaite, so the rest he placed with local farmers who willingly supported this arrangement. It may have been Peel, in fact, who first began the tradition of sending hounds back to their walks during the summer off-season in order to keep costs down. This arrangement, later copied by other fell packs, is still in place today, and it began forming during the early part of the nineteenth century. It drastically reduced the costs of maintaining a pack and only pregnant and nursing bitches remained in kennel during summertime.

Some of Peel's hunts were long and his hounds were very swift. One of Peel's hunts began close to the village of Caldbeck, in low-lying land, where hounds struck a drag which took them onto the Caldbeck Fells where at last Charlie was seen. Over this bleak and wild country ran the hounds, their music keeping the followers in touch, with John Peel riding his pony hard and getting across country as best he could. Over Uldale Charlie now took them and to the heights of massive Skiddaw, where Peel was forced to abandon his pony.

Hounds had already been hunting for well over two hours and Reynard now took to the vast slopes of Skiddaw again and kept hounds busy as they stuck determinedly to a holding line, their music audible as far away as the small town of Keswick. Hounds finally began to press their fox hard and they finally rolled him over in fine style out on the open fellside. He proved to be a fine dog fox of 16lbs and had kept Peel's hounds running for most of the day.

Peel would go to a nearby inn for 'refreshments' after such days among the hills and fells, and it seems he didn't see to his hounds first, which suggests he may well have had a Whipper-in (unpaid, as Peel could not afford staff) who would take them back to their lodgings, or back to kennel if hunting locally. Or Peel simply allowed his hounds to wander home of their own accord (this wasn't unusual with the less 'fashionable' packs in those days). Those trencher-fed hounds would find their way back to the farms where they were kept, whilst the others would return to kennels and no doubt be let in by one of Peel's children or his wife. He may also have had arrangements with innkeepers who would put them into one of the outbuildings until Peel was ready for home. He probably used a mix of such arrangements, depending on circumstances.

Whilst I was on holiday in the Lake District, staying at Ambleside in the heart of the Coniston Hunt country, I met an old chap who recalled hunting with Joe Bowman when the famous Ullswater Foxhounds Huntsman was towards the end of his career and they enjoyed many a celebration at *The Travel-*

Arthur Irving, stickmaker and ex-huntsman of the Eskdale & Ennerdale foxhounds.

lers Rest, which is now known as *The Kirkstone Pass Inn*. It was during a post-hunt celebration here that Bowman, who was only a boy when Peel died, said that he had been told John Peel was cruel with his hounds.

He was possibly a little neglectful if, after hunting, he headed straight for an inn and remained there for long periods without first seeing to his hounds, or making arrangements for them to be cared for in his absence. But cruel? His hounds were certainly fed well because, as reports show, they were clearly fit, sticking to a line all day, and into the night if necessary. They took part in many a long hunt, over time and distance.

Eyewitness accounts state that Peel's hounds were devoted to him and that farmers keeping hounds for him had to be careful when Peel was going hunting, for, upon hearing the sound of his horn, they would jump through a window to get to him, if doors were shut.

Many have stated that the image of Peel riding around country lanes, blowing his horn on a hunting morning, is one put about by 'romantics', but this was indeed the case. It was standard procedure with trencher-fed packs. Fred Barker, Master and Huntsman of the early Pennine Foxhounds, used to climb a hill close to his farm and blow on his horn until all the local hounds were loosed and soon joined him on a hunting morning. So Peel did practise this method and farmers made sure their hounds were loose first thing in a morning. Would hounds show such devotion and work so hard for a cruel man?

Peel hunted hounds fanatically for over fifty years on an income of less than £400 per year and Woodcock-Graves wrote that he was no businessman. During his later years he got into financial difficulties, but fund-raising events such as evening singsongs in local inns helped raise enough cash to keep hounds going. Peel's pack had a devoted following, from the northern fells to southern Scotland. Jackson Gillbanks of Whitefield, a man who hunted with Peel and who also composed a song about him, wrote that Peel had drawn every covert in the county and that he was well-known in the Scottish borders too. Peel's hunting ranged far and wide and hunted what is now the Ullswater, the Blencathra, the Melbreak, the Cumberland Farmers and the Cumberland Hunt countries, either in part, or in total, and his hunts sometimes reached to the west Cumberland coastline.

There are records of Peel hunting near Whitehaven only a few years before his death and on this day a carted deer was the quarry, which indicates that foxes and possibly hares too, were scarce at the time. A 'carted' deer was a tame one, which was taken to a chosen spot then released for the purpose of hunting. It was never killed and was taken back to be hunted another day.

Bagged foxes were also hunted on occasion and this practise was obviously cruel, but those were different times and carted deer and bagged foxes were commonly hunted throughout the country.

The practice was the same with 'bagged' fox but while the carted deer was picked up unharmed at the end of a hunt, the bagged foxes were usually killed. If they were saved during one hunt, then they were usually killed during the next and it must have been torture for the poor beasts involved.

Peel was a fit man throughout his life until his first and only illness, which killed him on Monday 13 November 1854 aged 78. He was buried in the churchyard at Caldbeck and was mourned by his wife, eleven surviving children and numerous grandchildren, as well as hundreds of friends.

He had hunted hounds for over fifty years in some of the roughest terrain in the country, rising at four or five each morning. After his death, Jackson Gillbanks wrote the beautiful song, *The Horn of the Hunter,* which is as follows:

For forty long years we have known him
A Cumberland yeoman of old
But twice forty years they shall perish
Ere the fame of his deeds shall grow cold.

Chorus:
The horn of the hunter is silent
By the banks of the Ellen no more
Nor in Denton is heard its wild echo
Clear sounding o'er the dark Caldew's roar.

No broadcloth, nor scarlet adorned him
Nor buckskins that rival the snow
But of plain Skiddaw gray was his raiment
He wore it for work, not for show.

Joe Wear (right) and the Whip Maldwyn Williams at a Mardale shepherds' meet (see Chapter 5, page 91).

But when darkness of night draws her mantle
And the cold round the fire bids us steal
Our children will say "Father come tell us
Some tales about famous John Peel."

And we'll tell them of Ranter and Royal
Of Briton and Bellman so true
How they rattled their fox around Carrock
And pressed him from chase into view.

And how often from Brayton to Skiddaw
Thro' Isel, Bewaldeth, Whitefiel'
We galloped like madmen together
To follow the hounds of John Peel.

Though long may we hunt with another
When the hand of old age we may feel
We'll mourn for a sportsman and brother
And remember the tales of John Peel.

Peel was instrumental in the development of the fell packs as he had consistently demonstrated that hunting hounds could be carried out in the fell country on a limited budget, provided farmers and villagers would assist by walking hounds and taking them back into their care through the summer months.

Peel didn't have paid hunt staff, though he had willing assistance for certain, but the fell packs began having both professional Huntsmen and Whippers-in, only being paid during the season itself, and with the hounds 'trencher-fed' during the summer, and only kennelled during the hunting season, all in order to reduce costs.

The Melbreak was the first of the fell packs to have a proper, organised structure with a professional Huntsman, Whipper-in and kennels; and the Coniston and Blencathra soon followed, with the Eskdale and Ennerdale Packs amalgamating and the Matterdale and Patterdale packs becoming the Ullswater, during the latter half of the nineteenth century. Their structure and their hounds were based on Peel's pack to some extent and, on the death of Peel, the Blencathra and Melbreak in particular had hounds from Peel's establishment. The best stud hounds from all the hunts were crossed with bitches from all the other Lake District packs. The Cumberland Hunt, for example, had hounds from Peel's pack when Wilfred Lawson bought several of Peel's hounds when they were sold after Peel's death.

So Peel lives on in these packs, the songs written about him, and in the hunting traditions still to be found in the Lake District. In fact, though hunting is mainly carried on via 'shank's pony' in the fells, there have been times when horses have been used and, before car following became a viable option to those even on limited incomes, all of the fell packs, the Coniston in partic-ular, enjoyed a certain amount of mounted followers, especially whenever hunting in the low country, with bridleways and country lanes, as well as farm tracks, being used to get about in order to keep in touch with hounds.

The Melbreak hunted quite a bit of low country and they enjoyed a few mounted followers before roads became too busy to make this possible any longer. In fact, the Melbreak country sported a number of excellent hunt and point to point horses and some of the regular mounted followers of the Cumberland Hunt would also follow the Melbreak whenever possible, with some being mounted.

5

LAKE DISTRICT SHEPHERDS' MEETS

Shepherds' Meets have an ancient history in the Lake District and these were traditionally held in order for stray sheep to be reunited with their proper owners. Sheep sometimes strayed far and wide and farmers would travel long distances, sometimes right to the other end of the fell country, in order to locate their lost sheep. Appointed shepherds would round up strayed sheep (identified by their brand marks) from surrounding fells; a job that could take two or three days prior to the Shepherds' Meet, and these sheep would be separated into flocks which would then be looked over by visiting shepherds.

Such events were usually held by a local inn and the *Kirkstone Pass Inn*, formerly known as *The Traveller's Rest*, was once one of the most famous of all locations for these annual occasions which were considered as very important among dalesfolk.

Along with this reuniting of stray sheep, hare and fox hunts were then held at the various Shepherds' Meets, and very often a hound trail was staged too. This is were a scent is artifically laid by a man along a set route, and special trail hounds (usually slimmer and faster than the normal fellhounds, although some hunts would enter a few working hounds too) would race along the scent, with a prize for the winner. Bets were often taken on the outcome.

Hound trailing was traditionally held during the summer months, but many trails were also staged in conjunction with

Shepherds' Meets during the winter and some of them were over a long distance, covering up to twelve miles. Fell-sides in deep-cut valleys were often the venue for the laid trail, so that a good view could be enjoyed by the spectators of hounds working out the line. Aniseed oil mixed with paraffin was used for the scent and nowadays, in inclement weather, engine oil is added to the mix in order to make the scent more 'holding'.

Many fell hunting folk kept a trail hound or two and in Victorian times, Hawkshead Solicitor William Heelis, the husband of Beatrix Potter, was a keen hound trailer and supporter of the Coniston Foxhounds. Some excellent hunting was enjoyed at these important and popular occasions and afterwards food and drink, along with song and dance, was enjoyed, sometimes into the early hours of the morning. Hunting the fox was a great social occasion, as well as an effective means of pest control,

This fox was bolted from an earth by Anthony Chapman's terrier, close to the Queen's Head, Troutbeck. The hounds lost it soon after this photo was taken.

Doug Paisley puts his terrier into rocky ground at Rigg (1930).

in this part of the world and the celebrations were just as important as the hunting itself. Most of the Lake District inns have witnessed great celebrations across the past two or three centuries and many are still used today for social events that are connected to the local fell packs.

The Mardale Shepherds' Meets had become the most important gathering in the Lake District, but all this came to an end when, in the late 1920s, work began on enlarging Lake Haweswater so that the growing sprawl of Manchester could be provided with necessary drinking water. This work sounded the death-knell of Mardale village itself and its incredibly popular meets when the area was flooded. Mardale Shepherds' Meets continued to be staged, but later in nearby villages and never again on the same scale.

During the 1929/30 season the Ullswater staged the last of the *in situ* Mardale Shepherds' Meets. Braithwaite Wilson was Huntsman at the time, with Joe Wear whipping-in. Perhaps it was the popularity of Joe Bowman who had previously made these meets so well supported, and folk travelled from miles

The Blencathra pack runs a fox to ground.

around to enjoy a week of hunting in this bleak and isolated area. Joe Bowman's name was synonymous with Mardale meets and songs were written about them, one in 1904 by Winson Scott, who regularly attended these meets and hunted with Bowman. The Mardale Hunt has long been a popular song:

The Mardale Hunt

The morn' is here awake my lads, away, away.
The hounds are giving mouth my lads, away my lads, away.
The Mardale Hunt is out today,
Joe Bowman strong shall lead the way,
Who ne'er has led his hunt astray, away my lads, away.

Our Bowman is a Huntsman rare, away, away.
His tally-ho's beyond compare, away my lads, away.
We always find him just the same,
At Grasmere Sports you'll hear his name,
His Mardale hunts will live in fame, away my lads, away.

The Mardale pack is on the trail, away, away.
The fox is leading thro' the dale, away my lads, away.
Hound Miller's on the scent, I'm told,
So foot it lads thro' frost and cold,
The mountain breeze is pure as gold, away my lads, away.

On Branstree Fell the fox is seen, away, away.
The hounds are off, the scent is keen, away my lads, away.
'Tis music sweet to t'dalesman's ear,
When hounds give mouth so loud and clear,
So off my lads and lend a cheer, away my lads, away.

The air is keen, our hearts are light, away, away.
We scale with glee the frowning height, away my lads away.
The fox has slipped and made his cave,
So in we send the terrier brave,
The fox will bolt, his brush to save, away my lads, away.

Our terrier frail will win or die, away, away.
So too will Wallow Crag say I, away my lads, away.
On Roman Fell in mountain cave,
We lost, alas, a terrier brave,
For good old Frisk we failed to save, away my lads, away.

Who'd weary with a sport like this? Away, away.
Or who a Mardale hunt would miss? Away my lads, away.
Our hardy fellsmen, hunters born,
Will rally to the Huntsman's horn,
Nor heeded be by rain or storm, away my lads, away.

Who'd hunt the fox with spur and rein? Away, away.
To have a mount we'd all disdain, away my lads, away.
We love our hills, our tarns, our fells,
We ken our moors, our rocks, our dells,
We love our hounds, we love oursel's, away my lads, away.

When darkness comes to Mardale, hie, away, away.
For who the Dunbull would decry? Away my lads, away.
Hal Usher kind will find a bed,
To rest our limbs and lay our head,
We're welcomed, housed, warmed and fed, away my lads, away.

In winter Mardale's drea and drear, away, away.
But 'tis not so if t'hunt is here, away my lads, away.
We trencher well, we trencher long,
We meet in dance, we meet in song,
For days are short and nights are long, away my lads, away.

We're lads from east and lads from west, away, away.
And north and south, all of the best, away my lads, away.
With Auld Lang Syne and Old John Peel,
With foaming glass and nimble heel,
We'll drink to all a-health and we'll away my lads, away.

The last time the Mardale Shepherds' Meet was held in the village, just prior to the flooding, Joe Bowman was absent due to ill-health. Manchester Corporation workmen were busy preparing the lake expansion whilst upwards of one hundred sheep were penned and inspected by local shepherds who were examining 'smit' (brand) marks that would identify those strays that belonged to their particular flocks.

Three local shepherds, T. Edmondson and R. Ebdell together with 'Tot' Greenhow (who was the Thronthwaite Hall and Naddle shepherd), had worked hard at gathering in all of these sheep and each one was successfully identified and allocated to their 'heffs' or 'hefts' (the area in which they should graze).

This was a tradition that went back centuries and in the Lake District, the Shepherds' Meet at Mardale Village had always staged the gathering of stray sheep to be reunited with their proper owners. But in 1929, crowbars, picks and shovels dislodged stone and shifted tons of earth in order to create a vast bowl that would take massive amounts of water. While this was going on, the last Mardale Hunt took place and while hounds were speaking to the line of a fox roused out on the open fell, the music of the hounds was drowned out by the blasting going on down below.

On the Saturday in question, hounds were unkennelled during fine weather, but rain quickly drifted in and began to fall as only rain can fall in that part of the world. A large field was in attendance and Mr A. Metcalfe-Gibson, the Master, and C.R. 'Kitty' Farrer, the Secretary, were among the glad throng. Sadly, Moore Sedgwick of Sedbergh, one-time Huntsman of

Joe Bowman arrives in style by carriage for a Mardale Shepherds' Meet, 1922.

The Melbreak pauses at Loweswater. Willie Irving, Huntsman (left), Harry Hardisty, Whipper-in (far right).

the Sedbergh Hounds, had just died and his presence was also missed, as he had been in regular attendance for many years.

Scent proved good after they had hit off a drag, and hounds soon unkennelled a fine dog fox at Riggindale. Two other foxes were also roused and one provided a superb hunt that took them all the way to Harter Fell, by way of High Street and Blea Water, where it went to ground and was left unmolested, probably because hounds had left followers far in the rear. The first fox was hunted around the Haweswater Valley in driving rain and was eventually run into (caught) on the fell not far from the little church at Mardale Village.

A hound trail was then enjoyed, as was customary during such special meets, with eleven hounds taking part. It is reported that Latrigg won this trail, but only just, finishing less than a yard in front of four other hounds competing for the finish line.

A sheepdog trial was also conducted on Mardale Village Green and was won by Mr Bennet's dog from Ambleside, while Mr Metcalfe of Borrowdale owned the dog that claimed second place.

After hunting and all of these other activities that made a Shepherds' Meet so special, rounds of beef, ham and herdwick mutton was enjoyed in the dining room and later the assembled hunters were entertained by Mr W. Skelton of Ambleside, who played piano as songs and rhyme went merrily round.

Another hunt was held that Saturday, which saw hounds loosed at nearby Riggindale and a large crowd was once again in attendance, with many out on the open fell watching the quarry as it stole away. Hounds hit off a drag near Chapel Hill Farm, which took them through Holme Pasture Breast, with Charlie being roused at Long Stile. He led them through some of the roughest country imaginable, consisting of rock, scree and crag, all of which are obstacles cunningly used by foxes in an attempt to keep pursuers at bay, with the aim of shaking them off.

This area was formerly known for holding a 'sweetmart' (pinemarten) if a fox couldn't be found, but by the late 1920s pinemartens were few and far between and the chance of finding foxes was far greater. Reynard took them under High Street, then doubled back and ran down the dale by Hugh Holme and back to Holme Pasture. He now made for the crags and managed to dodge hounds for a time, but they gradually began making ground on him and he was eventually driven to ground at a rocky den in the craggy fellside. A brace of terriers were put into this earth, but the account doesn't state which they were.

At this period 'Kitty' Farrer had his famous Gyp and Braithwaite Wilson had Crab and Crest, two of his best workers. Sid Wilkinson owned the superb finding and bolting terrier, Ullswater Nettle, and no doubt Joe Wear owned a good terrier or two by this time too. Fred Barker had some useful terriers and his 'Chowt-faced' Rock would possibly still be alive and working in 1929. So exactly which terriers were used on this occasion is impossible to say, though at least one of the above would have been in action that day. The terriers soon found and engaged their fox, but Charlie found things a little too hot to handle below ground, so he elected to bolt and was rolled over after a short but fast run.

A Monday meet was held at Mardale, after the Saturday gathering just described, and hounds hunted Whelter in unfavourable weather for hunting. A dense mist hung onto the tops of the High Street range of mountains and this, followers knew, could hamper proceedings. Braithwaite Wilson cast off his hounds at Castle Crag, with Joe Wear already out on the tops, and they quickly hit off a cold drag (on a scent trail but with no sight of the fox) that took them under Birch Crag, through Dry Syke and to Red Screes, where a grand 'racy' fox was afoot.

A fast run of fifty minutes ensued with hardly a check! They went through Iron Gutter and over the tops into Wrangdale, then on to Kidsty Pike at the head of Riggindale. The winds up here were very strong and such a powerful force turned Charlie. He now went with the wind across the top of Rampsgill, over High Raise and along the edge of Martindale for quite some distance. Conditions were difficult to say the least, but the grand swell of hound music rising and falling with the strong winds helped keep Huntsmen and followers in touch.

On through Pots an' Pans to Keys Ghyll at the head of Fusedale and Charlie now made back in the direction of Mardale by way of Long Grain, Measend Beck and to the head of Forrenda. Reynard kept on and hounds followed relentlessly, going by way of Broad Seves to Whelter again.

Hounds were gaining on a flagging fox by now and they pressed him down under Basin Crag and across the swollen beck raging down the steep mountainside. Twenty hounds, with Clara leading them, now pushed their fox to Devil's Chimney, a steep, narrow gulley through the crags, which Reynard now attempted to climb. Hounds were too close, however, and they finally pulled him down under Woodie Crag. A fine dog fox of

Jim Dalton and George Bell with the Blencathra pack outside the Borrowdale Hotel in the late 1920s.

17lb had been accounted for after a superb hunt in incredibly difficult conditions. No doubt the *Dunbull Inn* rattled to some celebrations that night!

Hounds hunted again on the Tuesday, though only half the pack was deemed fit enough to take out. This was normally due to cut pads, which would cause the hound to limp and be declared lame. The morning had heavy showers of hail and so conditions were not too favourable yet again, not unusual in this part of the country. Braithwaite Wilson loosed his reduced pack at the hotel and Joe Wear climbed out to the higher tops as hounds hit off a drag, but the hail showers interfered with progress.

The trail took them along Branstree and to Woodford Ghyll, where Charlie was at last encountered. This was a game fox and it took them at quite a fast pace, despite rough weather and even rougher ground, forward over Gatesgarth Pass and to Harter Fell, which is one of the most dangerous of places for hounds to run.

Sheer-drop crags present many dangers to hounds and followers alike and their fox took them on a very rough course indeed, which sadly witnessed Rachel and Comfort, two superb Ullswater bitches, losing their footing as they attempted to follow across the crag face and falling 300ft down the cliffs. It was thought they would surely be dead, but, amazingly, they survived, though badly cut and bruised. Rachel had to be carried back to Mardale, but, incredibly, Comfort was able to walk back, if rather slowly and with a stiff gait. Their chances of survival were good, as long as there was no internal damage.

In the meantime the rest of the pack hunted on, going out onto the top of the fell without further mishap and on to Little Harter Fell, Lone Moss Folds and back into Branstree. They now climbed out over the tops and made for Mosedale, going right down this valley to Swindle. They eventually left this vale and now made out for Black Bells, going some distance towards Naddle Forest, and on towards Mardale Bank. The fox then swung left-handed and took the oncoming pack through Branstree again, with hounds finally catching and killing their quarry, a fine vixen, in Edmund's Lot. This hunt finished meets at Mardale for that week and this vixen was the twenty-first fox accounted for that season, with nine having been taken in the past fortnight at Longsleddale, Kentmere and, of course, Mardale. All nine were taken by hounds in the open, though terriers had been needed in order to bolt some of them. The Ullswater pack was obviously in fine fettle.

Alfred Wainwright, that great fell walker, writer and artist, lamented the 'passing' of Mardale Village, known affectionately as Mardale Green when it was eventually inundated with water in the early 1930s and ever afterwards he declared the flooded

Joe Mear and Joe Wilkinson lead the Ullswater pack through Penrith. Town centre meets like this in the 1930s would often attract several hundred followers.

Johnny Richardson and his Whip Bill Porter with the Blencathra in the early 1950s.

valley a 'sad sight'. How much sadder was it to those who once attended the famous Mardale Shepherds' Meets and enjoyed such great hunting, exciting hound trails and tense sheepdog trials, not to mention the evening celebrations that often went on well into the night, with good food, drink, games, songs and rhymes creating a cheerful atmosphere in the lonely village inn?

6

HUNTING THE FOX

All-out war was once waged against the fox population of the Lake District, against predators and vermin, and it wasn't until the time of John Peel that the 'sporting' potential of foxes was realised and a different view began to be taken of this animal.

Before Peel, they were simply viewed as vermin to be caught by any means possible and the bounty system in place until the latter half the nineteenth century meant that several farmers and professional pest controllers made part of their living by killing such beasts, which were troublesome to those who reared livestock.

This bounty system ensured that a tradition grew in the fells of hounds and terriers being kept at most farms throughout the Lake District and even in some of the towns such as Keswick, Egremont and Kendal.

Terriers were just as important as hounds and until about the 1890s, terriers would run as part of the pack. Hounds would stick to a cold drag for hours at a time, provided a severe storm, or strong sunshine, didn't make scent impossible, until they reached where the fox was lying up. The terriers were then entered and the fox bolted and shot, or it was killed in the earth by the terriers and dug out.

Polecats, otters, badgers and pinemartens, as well as wildcats before they became extinct in the fells, met similar fates and Church Wardens would pay out for either the carcass, or the tails of predators accounted for (hence the need to dig out a dead carcass). Hedgehogs were also on the quarry list at one time and this may explain why many Fell, Lakeland and Patterdale terriers (all of which share the same ancestry) can often be driven crazy by the scent of hedgehog. I like hedgehogs and regard them as a type of pest controller in that they eat slugs and snails and are thus an ally of keen gardeners and crop growers, but, alas, they also rob ground nests of eggs and so they became unpopular with gamekeepers and the gentry. So these too were considered fair game in the fell country.

However, John Peel showed great enthusiasm for hound work, rather than for simply catching and killing predators and

Gone to ground: the Lunesdale pack and Huntsman Paul Whitehead are delayed on an open stretch of moorland.

claiming bounty on them, as well as enjoying the social side of the hunt. Others such as Squire Crozier and William Pearson began to follow Peel's lead and gather small packs together and from the early part of the nineteenth century more emphasis was placed on hound work, though fox control remained an important part of hunting. In fact, predator control was still an important focus in Peel's time and foxes, otters, badgers, polecats and pinemartens continued to be hunted, though other quarry was usually sought only if a fox couldn't be found. Keepers also remained keen with the gun and foxes were regularly shot, so they were rather scarce in those days.

It wasn't until after the Second World War that the number of gamekeepers declined and far less shooting was carried out, which has meant a more healthy and prosperous fox population in the fells from the 1940s, and it was fell hunting that guaranteed this healthy population.

Foxes have only ever been tolerated in the Lake District for one reason only: so that hounds could hunt the different areas and provide a great social life for farmers, villagers and townsfolk alike, while at the same time providing a means to continue protecting livestock. If it were not for the fell packs, then foxes would not be tolerated at all and wholesale control would be the order of the day.

This was not taken into account when the hunting ban was passed in 2004. I am not against the shooting of foxes and know that it has its place in modern pest control when carried out in a responsible manner, but I was recently reading of over forty foxes being shot in one night and this can in no way provide a selective form of control, which is what was accomplished when using hounds.

Not all foxes prove troublesome to livestock. The beauty of hunting with hounds was that the troublesome fox, as reported by a land-owner, was often hunted down and accounted for.

Troublesome foxes were the main target of the hunt, and hounds would be called in when poultry, ducks and geese, as well as lambs, were being worried. And this sometimes occurred in more built-up areas. For instance, there are accounts of foxes killing geese and hens at Ambleside, one such incident being at the *Salutation Hotel* when the Landlord had his fattening birds killed, and the Coniston Foxhounds were called in to deal with the problem.

Hounds would be taken to the area, the scent was then taken up and followed to where Reynard rested, or in the early days, perhaps where a polecat lay, and then a hunt would begin and the predator be accounted for, it was hoped. In the early years when bounties were paid, all efforts were made to recover the carcass and this tradition continued even into our modern day, despite the fact that no monies could be claimed for proof of a kill.

Even after terriers had emerged, huge digs have occurred, sometimes lasting for days, just to recover the body of a dead fox, which was often hung from an old wooden beam and toasted at a local inn. The *Kirkstone Pass Inn*, the *Queen's Head* at Troutbeck, the *Fish Inn* at Buttermere, the *Kirkstile Inn* at Loweswater, the *King George* at Eskdale, both the *Salutation Inn* and *Horse and Farrier* at Threlkeld, the *White Lion* at Patterdale and *The Ship Inn* at Coniston are just a few of the hostelries once associated with such celebrations and many have been the occasions when successful hunts and the carcass of a fox have been toasted at these famous places.

Famous foxhounds

Some individual hounds have made great names for themselves and one of these was Butler of the Melbreak pack, who was

Walter Parkin leading his Lunesdale hounds out of Hawes in February 1951 (see also picture on page 16).

walked by John Newby of Loweswater. Hounds were drawing on the fells south of Buttermere when Butler slunk away on his own and roused a fox on Dodd Level. Reynard set his mask for High Stile and took two circuits round this district, but, being hard-pressed by this lone hound, the fox made across the fellsides above Buttermere and onto Melbreak Fell, round Piel Hill and to the foot of Crummock Water.

He then doubled back, trying to make out for the high fells again, but was turned down Mosedale and eventually made out for the lowlands instead. He took a dip in the beck at High Nook and was here tally-ho'd by John Walton, which sent him on his way for Holme Wood, where he was saluted by Thomas Rawling and J. Wilkinson.

On past Holme House the fox and lone hound sped and to the top of the Force, then back round by the wood. Johnny Pearson of Rannerdale now sent him on his way with ringing

cheers and Butler the hound was spurred on by the encourage-
ment, despite the long distance and exertions of it all.

He next made by Wateryeat, after spending a bit of time in
and out of woodland, and headed for the river at Loweswater
and here he crossed, making over the lowland fields to Foulsyke
Wood and then to Potter Ghyll, heading for the fells once more.
He then took to covert and awaited his foe, hoping to have shaken
him off, but on came the tenacious Butler so Reynard moved on
yet again, making back to Foulsyke, where, finally, the hound
caught him briefly, but Reynard broke away and made across
the fields, only to be caught again soon after. Butler worried

*Willie Irving (fourth from right) and Melbreak hunt followers near
Whinlatter.*

Willie Irving assembles his Melbreak hounds in Cockermouth town centre, a meet that always attracted a good crowd.

this fox unaided and thus became one of the great Melbreak hounds noted for being able to hunt alone and unassisted. His quarry on this occasion proved a fine dog fox of 16lbs weight and the carcass was stuffed by a Mr D. Linton and was presented by Jonathan Banks, the ex-Huntsman of the Melbreak to Ted Newby, who was in at the kill with A. Swinburn. This lone hunt had lasted for three hours fifteen minutes.

Another Melbreak hunt saw lone hounds at work and this was after a meet at the *Horse Shoe Inn*, Lorton, where Mrs Benson was famous for her hospitality, as well as her hound and terrier walking which stretched back to the time of Jonathan Banks and Squire Benson.

This hunt was during Huntsman Willie Irving's reign and the day was rather unpromising, with heavy mist on the fells. A large crowd gathered at the inn, however, and all headed for the first draw, which was in the low country, due to mist on higher ground. Hounds were loosed near Gilbrea and quickly found on the lower reaches of the fells. Reynard rapidly made for Harrot and through Wilson Wood, then for Kirkfell and across to the Wythop district, where several more foxes were afoot and here the pack divided.

It was hard going keeping in touch with unfolding events and now the dense mist set in, with only the haunting sound of baying hounds guiding hunt staff and followers. After a while, however, the mist drifted out across the tops allowing over half an hour of fine hound work to be seen before the mist set in again, worse than ever.

After some time the hound Delver could be seen hunting a fox single-handedly, going at a rattling pace across Sunny Brows and into Rash Wood. On he sped and eventually overhauled his fox, killing it in Whit Beck just above The Tenters. Next Laddie was seen running over Swinside in pursuit of a fox he had roused from the Bottoms. He made over to Whiteside and to Gasgale Ghyll, for Dove Crags, with never a check.

Reynard took Laddie all the way to the craggy breast of Grasmoor and then headed down for the low country, crossing the fields at Lanthwaite Green. Laddie pushed his quarry hard here and finally killed his fox, a fine dog, near Beck House on the Buttermere road.

The ground covered was exceedingly rough and the hunt a spectacular one. As most were making back to the inn to enjoy the hospitality of Mr and Mrs Geldart, a final hunt was still in progress as hounds raced after their fox to Sunny Brows and to Kirkfell, now going down the crags to Kirkfell House, where a bull terrier joined in the chase and helped catch and kill a third fox for the day. Celebrations went on well into the night back at the Horseshoe Inn, which is now a private residence.

Once the 'sporting' potential of foxes was realised and popularised by such stalwarts as John Peel and Squire Crozier, they became the principal quarry of Lakeland hunts and

An illustration from Dalesman's book depicting half fox, half hare hunter.

Foxhound blood was introduced into some of the many existing harrier packs found throughout the region, who concentrated on hunting the hare. This produced the faster, more agile hounds which were necessary for hunting on the rough slopes and peaks of the Lake District mountains.

The Blencathra had become a famous pack during Crozier's time, noted for some wonderful hunts. One such was on Skiddaw, after a start was made at Brundholme End, and the drag took them to Horseshoe Crag, where Reynard showed them his heels. He took them to Black Wood on Latrigg and here another fox was afoot, which, as was often the case, split the pack.

The first hunt took one lot of hounds through the breast of Windy Brow, where they got sight of him and were soon on excellent terms. They coursed him to Horseshoe Crag and there pulled him down after a fast hunt. The remainder of the hounds meanwhile chased their second fox by Burr Ghyll, Applethwaite

The Blencathra at Watendlath in the 1930s.

Ghyll, to the top of Jenkin, then back by Whitbeck. On now through Lonscale Fell and Combe Ghyll, then away to Saddle-back, before coming back to Lonscale Fell.

Hounds were going at a rattling pace with a 'screaming' scent all the way, pressing him very hard indeed. Compelled by the pressure hounds put him under, the fox now went to earth in a borran at Brunt Horse and a terrier was soon on to him, with followers hoping he would bolt.

However, Reynard chose to stay and make a fight of it, so digging commenced and some large boulders had to be removed before, at last, their quarry was seen being worried by a game Blencathra terrier. Reynard was drawn out alive and set on his feet again, which was common practise in those days, and Ringwood led the pack as they hunted him to Brundholme Mines, where he was at last accounted for.

It seems rather unsporting to set a fox on its feet again after digging it out, but fell hunters would give Reynard a chance of escape whenever possible, even though not much lead or law was given, especially if the fox being hunted was a livestock-worrier, in order to put the odds in the hounds' favour. I do not have a date for the hunt described above, but it was likely to have been during George Bell's time as Huntsman (1930-1949), and very probably during the early 1930s.

High country 'greyhound' foxes

Much has been written about the so-called 'greyhound fox' said to inhabit the high country of the Lake District, which was of a distinct grey colouring and leaner, more agile and far more hardy than the 'lowland' foxes, most of which could be distinguished by their black legs. Such 'greyhound' foxes were said to be heavier too, tipping the scales at over 16lbs and often just over twenty. The truth is that in the old days, when most packs hunted hares, few foxes were actually found out on the high places. Those few who existed kept to the valleys where food sources were much more abundant, so it is unlikely that a distinct variety could have existed, as, even if foxes were found on the high mountain ranges (and a very few were), they would still seek a mate in the lowlands where far more foxes were found. Lowland and high country foxes would breed, and a mixed race would have resulted, thus watering down any possibility of a distinct variety in the centuries before packs of hounds were used in Cumberland, Westmorland and North Lancashire, where the fell packs operated.

When most packs switched to fox as their primary quarry, they began drawing through lowland pastures and woodlands on a regular basis and thus dispersed many foxes which began taking to the high country and thus, as the nineteenth century progressed, more and more began to be found on the fells and greater numbers took to the crags and rockpiles (borrans and bields) where they were safer.

I have no doubts that grey foxes existed, as they still do today, and that such foxes passed on their distinct colouring, but I do not believe that these were a strain of fox different to low country specimens. As there is variety in litters of puppies, so there is variety in litters of foxes and some would be rich red and black, while others would be of a poor red colouring generously smattered with grey.

Those that inhabited the high country were fleet of foot and in modern times such hardy runners have been encountered (I have witnessed hunts on particularly fast foxes myself, which have taken hounds great distances), but that was simply because of their fit condition. High country foxes are healthier because they come in contract with less disease and the long distances travelled in order to obtain food and find a mate mean that they are hard-muscled and extremely fit. In the old days a

Jim Dalton in the 1920s (see page 143). The Blencathra Huntsman had 'one speed, up hill and down dale – and it was a killer!'

diet of, among many other things, mutton (foxes eat dead sheep and kill lambs), rabbit and game birds (the Lake District was heavily keepered in those days) meant regular and plentiful food supplies and this explains why many foxes weighed 16lbs or more. Weights of 19lbs were quite common pre-1940s and this was true of black legged foxes too, so heavier weights do not equate to 'greyhound' foxes.

Joe Bowman hunted using around twelve or thirteen couple of hounds for most of his career with the Ullswater pack and with this number killed many hundreds, a lot of which were heavy. For instance, foxes he took from Crossfell averaged around 19lbs (hounds of the fell packs didn't break up their quarry and most carcasses were weighed) and one he took tipped the scales at well over 20lbs.

In 1899 the Ullswater were hunting locally when they ran a fox to ground at a borran at the foot of tall crags close to Ullswater Lake. Bowman put in one of his best terriers, Corby, and a terrific battle ensued indicating that Charlie had chosen to stay and make a fight of it. Digging tools were sent for and quickly employed, and tons of rock were shifted over a 24 hour period, with the game little terrier finally being uncovered. The carcass of a large fox had prevented her from getting out of the lair and this was removed and later weighed, tipping the scales at a whopping 23lbs. Incredibly, when the terrier Corby was pulled out of the borran, bitten from ear to ear and in a frightful state, two other large foxes, stone dead, like the first, were also discovered.

The little terrier bitch had killed three large foxes in that borran, with a combined weight of 62lbs! And Bowman once accounted for a fox on Crossfell with his Ullswater pack that also weighed in at 23lbs, which was the largest he ever caught in the Lake District.

Today's foxes

The fact is that heavy foxes have been accounted for in various different parts of the UK – a fox killed near Keith, in Scotland, weighed 21lbs. A brace killed in Argyllshire scaled 22 and 18lbs respectively. Terriers killed a fox near Beddgelert in Wales that tipped the scales at a massive 29lbs. In Oxfordshire, in the year 1900, hounds caught a very young fox that already weighed over 17lbs. Had it reached full maturity, it would surely have weighed over 20lbs. Most fell foxes accounted for were found to weigh between 14 and 19lbs.

Today we have fewer keepered estates, a short supply of rabbits in many areas due to recent disease, fewer sheep on the fells – and this all means less available food supplies for modern foxes, which generally do not reach the same weights as in those days of abundance, though the exceptional heavy foxes have been accounted for in more recent times too.

Far more foxes inhabit the fells these days, so there is far more of a chance of inbreeding and poorer specimens passing on their genes. In the old days, when foxes were hunted down ruthlessly, the surviving population was naturally the fittest. Diseased foxes were rarely found, so the fittest passed on their genes and generally produced good quality offspring that, with an abundant food supply and far less competition for those supplies, along with wider-ranging territories due to the smaller fox population, meant fit and hardy specimens which could give long runs and often escape in the end.

Nowadays, foxes are found in abundance so their territories

Johnny Richardson and Stan Mattinson at Latrigg.

Mike Fernhead, Whipper-in to the Lunesdale foxhounds, at Barn Farm in 1975.

are naturally much smaller, which means foxes patrol smaller areas and thus are not as fit as their ancestors. This means that more fall to hounds than was the case previously. Also, hounds are probably faster today than they were formerly, when heavy harrier blood made up quite a bit of the fellhound breeding.

Harrier blood was used to steady hounds, so that they would cast more patiently if they lost a scent line, or when 'dragging' as they worked up to where a fox lay. Hunting hares required hard, persistent work from hounds and foxhunters desired such qualities in their packs of fellhounds. This meant that at one stage they lost some of the speed which I believe had been introduced using running dog blood, when Scottish Todhunters came to the Lakes in order to claim bounties. With the cessation of bounties during the nineteenth century, more emphasis was put on hound work, rather than on catching quarry as quickly as possible, so those early hunters had had no qualms about bringing harrier blood into their packs.

It is logical to believe that modern hounds, being faster than those that were infused with the heavy harrier blood during Georgian and Victorian times, and with far less of an inclination to 'dwell' on a line, would be capable of catching their quarry more quickly. This has indeed been the case. There are of course exceptions to this rule, but generally speaking modern hunts are shorter in both time and distance.

In my opinion, reports of 'greyhound' foxes were a myth: the 'greyhound' fox caught during Squire Crozier's reign which I saw mounted in a glass case was no different to any other fox and was only as grey as quite a few modern foxes I have seen.

White foxes are far rarer than grey foxes and I can find records of only three having been accounted for nationwide: one with the Beaufort Hunt in 1915; one with the Taunton Vale Foxhounds at Cothelstone, Somerset in 1886; and one with the Ullswater Foxhounds in more recent times, this being the fox on which I based my novel, *The White Fox of Withersrush Moor*. A white fox was roused by the Devon and Somerset Staghounds during the 1880/81 season and a few of the followers viewed it away.

Heavy foxes: an Ullswater event

All of the fell packs have accounted for quite heavy foxes over the years and one of the gamest was hunted by the Ullswater in 1937. Joe Wear loosed his hounds at Hartsop and a drag was immediately struck, which took them to Heck Crag, where Joe Wilkinson, the brother of Sid and son of Jonathon, the Ullswater Whipper-in at that time, had climbed out, on the lookout for Reynard leaving his daytime retreat. Their fox was indeed skulking at this crag, but he swiftly left and made out for Riggindale at the head of Haweswater, after going by Buck Crag and High Seat.

Hounds quickly picked up the line, cheered on by those following in their wake, and the glorious swell of music signalled good scenting. The pack streamed away in a long line of black, tan and white. They now went across Mardale and climbed out as if making for Swindale, but Reynard suddenly turned instead for Naddle Forest. Hounds raced in his wake and began pressing their quarry severely, running with great ardour towards Thornthwaite Hall, then on to the low end of Swindale, where they finally broke into view and ran their quarry down.

He proved to be a big fellow of 18½lbs and he had given hounds a long, fast and hard hunt of three hours. He was a fine fell fox and had quite a bit of age to him, so he had probably shaken off his pursuers on a number of previous occasions.

A Blencathra hunt

The Blencathra had an exciting hunt about the same time and about 60 followers traversed the fellsides and awaited the presence of a fox as they stood scattered amongst the high tops in readiness of a find.

Hounds roused a fox from near Eagle Crag in Borrowdale and went off in pursuit, but for some reason, one of the hounds, Darling, refused to go with them and instead began 'feathering' (touching a light scent and wagging her tail) between Eagle Crag and Sergeant Crag, those two great pikes reaching into the sky.

Harry Hardisty with the Melbreak foxhounds and his famous terrier, Turk, in the foreground.

Suddenly she began speaking eagerly (baying) and went round Eagle Crag in pursuit of a fox she had roused single-handed. Reynard took her to Greenup Edge at a fast and furious pace and her music could be heard all around this wild and fearsome valley.

Darling now dropped down to Langstrath Beck and raced after her fox across rough rock and scree, her frustration evident to followers as she screamed in the wake, unable to get up sufficient speed over this dangerous country. She followed the beck for some distance, then crossed and went out of sight amongst the rough vastness of Glaramara and the end was not known, though it is thought Reynard made good his escape.

Meanwhile, the rest of the pack was hunting their fox on the top of Glaramara and Charlie swung left and went to ground at Wolf Ghyll. A brace of Blencathra terriers were entered and

A poignant moment as Spider the terrier is rescued after being trapped for six days underground in the Langdales, January 1934 (see page 209).

they quickly forced their quarry to bolt. Charlie ran down the fellside at top speed, hounds not being able to keep pace with him, and went to ground yet again. This time he was unwilling to face hounds anymore and was worried below ground by the terriers. It seems Darling had rejoined the pack by this time and they roused another soon after, which they accounted for on the Seathwaite side of Glaramara – a good day for the Blencathra!

A Melbreak hunt

In March 1927 Willie Irving was called out to deal with a poultry-worrying fox that was causing havoc near Cockermouth. A drag was hit off close to where the worrying had occurred and the Melbreak pack succeeded in finding and rousing their trouble-some fox on Dubs Moss. He seemed reluctant to head for the high ground and instead went to earth in a drain at Eaglesfield Crag. Irving put in one of his terriers: his best at that time included Riff, Floss, Blue Floss, Boss, Grip, Squib, Midge, Crab, Tim (walked by J. Allinson of Cockermouth), Felix, Peggy (bred out of Thomas Rawling's strain and the dam of Rawling's famous Gillert), Trig, Tinker and Sting. Any one of these could have been used that day, though Riff, Floss and Felix seem to have been used more than the others.

Reynard bolted rather swiftly from whichever Melbreak terrier it was, and now set his mask for the Loweswater fells. A rattling pace ensued and hounds spoke eagerly to a good line as they sped down the enchanting Lorton Vale and disappeared into the fells around Loweswater.

It took some time for followers to catch up and when they did, hounds were returning, showing signs that they had already worried their quarry. It was thought they caught him in the lake, but no carcass could be found. However, a few days later the outcome was at last discovered. Some boys out playing found the dead fox on the kitchen floor of an abandoned cottage at Crabtree Beck. He had obviously jumped through a broken window and had quickly been followed by the pack, with an obvious outcome. He was a game fell fox and had given hounds a terrific run.

Short hunts

Hounds very often killed after long hunts, some of them mammoth in time and distance, but occasionally short runs were enjoyed. The Ullswater met at Glencoyne one Monday morning in the early spring of 1927 and Braithwaite Wilson loosed his pack immediately after the meet at the farm. A drag was quickly struck and taken to the west-end of Black Crag, where at last Charlie was put up.

The day was mild, but the fell-tops were enveloped in mist, which could cause problems if Reynard made out for the heights. Hounds got away on excellent terms and drove their fox through Sheffield Pike, where a second fox took to his heels and divided the pack. Four hounds, Major, Leader, Miller and Towley gamely stuck to their original task, whilst the rest headed off in the wake of their second.

These four gallant hounds enjoyed a fast spin of 25 minutes after hunting him through Glenridding Screes, towards Stick Pass, then right-handed into Linkondale. Back by Old Wall Head now they headed and here he was viewed at last, with hounds pressing him hard and forcing him to attempt to cross the valley. However, Major, a hound well known at that time for speed and great hunting qualities, soon caught up with him and the eager quartet dealt with their fox behind a large rock near Seldom Seen Cottages. The brush of a fine dog fox was picked up by Miss Little.

Meanwhile, the other fox went by the screes, past Greenside

Willie Irving with his terrier Turk of Melbreak, 1931.

Mines, as if making for the wild heights of Helvellyn. However, the hunt swung left over Kepple Cove and Red Tarn Becks, for Linkondale, where Charlie took refuge in a sheer-drop crag and had to be left. This spot was deemed far too dangerous for hound or terrier to venture and so Reynard saved his brush by his cunning tactics.

The Coniston pack had a superb day's hunting in early December of 1934 when Ernie Parker was Huntsman, having taken over from George Chapman after he had been forced to retire in 1931 because of a niggling ankle injury sustained several years earlier whilst hunting in the Coniston district.

A fox was roused at Hawkshead and he took hounds around the lower country in the Elterwater district, before at last climbing out to higher ground at Lingmoor Dale End Crag. Away for Chapel Stile now they went, then back to the heights of surrounding mountains with the pack speaking eagerly in his wake as he led them across some of the roughest boulder-strewn country imaginable. This meant that he gained ground, despite

An early photo of the Rydal Hound Show.

the hounds expertise over this rough country and their haunting full-cry for blood sounded even higher as they reached the foot of Stake Pass where a heavy and wild storm blew up suddenly and the fox thus saved his brush, after a cracking long-distance hunt that took in many of the high mountains. A second fox was roused after Parker had gathered in his pack and the drag led out to Pull Scar where Charlie showed his heels.

He took them around Tarn Hows, through Yewdale Crags and all across the lower fells to Rydal, where he took to Nab Scar, which has featured in many a Coniston Foxhounds hunt. From here he led them to the heights of Fairfield above Grasmere and hounds rattled him all the way to Heron Crag where he went to ground, the pressure from the fleet pack compelling him to try his luck amongst the dark recesses of ancient piles of fallen rock.

Fortune didn't favour him, though, as terriers were entered, possibly Ernie Parker's wonderfully game dog, Turk, already a famous black terrier, playing a part in proceedings, as Reynard wouldn't bolt and so was worried below ground. Parker used Turk whenever Charlie refused to make for open ground, as this fiery-tempered earth dog was certain death to any fox reluctant to bolt. Parker's Turk was probably sired by his equally famous dog, Nigger, who was not only a great worker, but a grand-looking terrier too.

Mounted packs

Foot packs have been employed in the Lake District for generations, though in the areas of low country, these packs have enjoyed a certain amount of mounted following too. Peel used his fell ponies with hounds in the low country wherever possible, riding along the lanes, but some packs in the area were entirely mounted: the Cumberland Hunt; the Cumberland Farmers and the Oxenholme Staghounds – though all of these packs covered areas *surrounding* what is traditionally viewed as the Lake District.

The Cumberland Hunt cover the western side all the way to the Solway, which comprises mostly rolling hills and includes country hunted by John Peel, as it is ideal for mounted following. In 1934 the Cumberland Hunt had a good day after a meet at Dovenby Mill, despite poor conditions when mist was almost down to the ground.

The field consisted of Sir Wilfred Lawson (Master) Davies (Huntsman), Miss Parkin, Miss L. Fisher, Miss Young, Miss Pinkney, Mrs Bennet, G. James, J. Hetherington, C.F. Jackson, W. Young, C. Young and J. Littleton. Times were hard in the 1930s and so a number of unemployed folk from Dearham and Broughton were also out and no doubt following on foot.

The mist began to lift as hounds were loosed at Dovenby Gorse, where, typically, a fox was roused from this famously

One of the Blencathra terriers.

130

'smittle' spot (one likely to spark a 'find'). Hounds spoke almost immediately they were lead into covert and Reynard chose to exit the woods on the Dovenby side. The pack got away on good terms and ran him fast across the hilly pastures for Kellywell Covert, running the whole length of this place and exiting by Dovenby Crags, now crossing the Cockermouth-Maryport road and into Cow Crags pastures. He then crossed a stream and ran at full throttle into Dovenby Hall Park, skirting the hall then the village and through Duffenside Covert, making for Line Foot Station where he went to ground in a big drain by the side of the railway.

Mounted packs need good terriers as much as foot packs and the Cumberland Hunt have had their fair share, the very best of which was Turk of Bridekirk (several of the very best Lakeland terriers have been named Turk). He was celebrated in verse and he may well have been out of the Melbreak strain. Alternatively, in one of Willie Irving's notebooks, a reference is made to Jack, J. Hodgson's terrier, who was an ancestor of Irving's strain and Turk of Melbreak in particular, with a note stating that Jack was 'Turk's brother'.

Could this reference have been to Turk of Bridekirk? I can think of no other Turk that it could have been, unless Irving had Dalton's famous dog in mind, though a letter from the time states that Dalton's Turk was the sire of Hodgson's Jack. The fact that Willie Irving kept a copy of a hunting song celebrating Turk of Bridekirk may suggest there was some connection with the Melbreak. This is more than possible, since Allinson of Cockermouth walked terriers for the Melbreak even before Irving's time at the hunt. He also provided terriers for the Cumberland Hunt and carried out some of the terrier work for them, so the connection could have been through this. In any case, a Cumberland Hunt terrier, very likely descended from Turk of Bridekirk, was now entered into the drain and soon found the fox skulking below ground and quickly bolted it, with a fast chase now ensuing. At least two hounds got hold of him as he bolted, but he shook himself free on both occasions and eventually got away to a greenhouse in a nearby garden while the hounds overran.

However, on casting back they roused him from this shelter and he circled the area, no doubt with the intent of getting to ground again, but was prevented by hounds severely pressing him. And so away he went, back on almost his exact line to Dovenby Gorse, with hounds running well on a holding scent.

They forced him from the gorse yet again and he now made out by Bonny Hill, running past the farmstead and over the road past Gate House and to the main Carlisle-Cockermouth road to Wood Hall. It was here that this game, hard-run fox saved his brush, as a fresh one jumped up in front of hounds and the Huntsman could not prevent them from changing.

This fresh fox raced back to Dovenby Gorse and away past the mill and school before finally running hounds out of scent in the neighbourhood of Dovenby Station. But this had been a rattling good hunt over beautiful country and the hounds performed incredibly well, with a spectacular bolt from a big drain thrown in for good measure. It had been a cracker of a hunt and was more than worthy of note.

The song celebrating Turk of Bridekirk was written in 1937 by John W. Lewthwaite in Toronto, Canada, where he seems to have emigrated after leaving Cumberland.

The words suggest the writer carried out much of the terrier work for the hunt at that time and goes as follows:

Tally ho, tally ho, what a heart-stirring cry,
I would like to hear it today.
And feel like I used to when Big Bill and I,
Went foxhunting Sunny-Brows way.

With Old Grip and Tar, the best terriers out,
And as keen as the liveliest hound.
We always contrived to be there, or about,
In case brier-fox ran to ground.

If so and the terriers failed in their work,
Through vixen's too hostile affront,
Jack Wilson would gallop to Bridekirk for Turk,
The pride of the Cumberland Hunt.

But cast no reflection on Tar, or Old Grip,
Nor class a bold fox with a mole.
Jack knew his dog-kingdom and so did the Whip,
Turk sure was their ace in the hole.

Yes, sir, and today I am pleased to confess,
Old foxes in safest of grounds,
Paid regular tribute to Turk's gameliness,
By taking a chance with the hounds.

Tally ho, tally ho, was the general cry,
The thought of it thrills me today,
The same as it did when Big Bill would reply,
"Hark forrard, yoo-hoo, gone away."

The scarlet-clad Huntsmen, the sound of the horn,
The spankiest mounts in the land,
The stirring hound music, a fine crispy morn,
Was anything ever so grand?

This, framed in the wild glaring beauty around,
Viewed wholly, or only in part,
I verily swear was sufficient to pound,
A song in the stoniest heart.

No wonder 'John Peel' is still heartily sung,
Without any kindred regret.
No wonder we Cumbrians love to give tongue,
To what we can never forget.

A Cumberland Hunt from the meet to the kill,
Regardless of where, or how far,
Love to remember, if just for the thrill
Of thinking of Bill, Grip and Tar.

Old Grip and Tar were obviously extensively used at the Cumberland Hunt and were normally very useful for bolting foxes, but if Charlie got himself into a strong place from where he would not bolt, then that ace in the hole of Bridekirk was sent for. He could shift reluctant foxes from deep strongholds where it was impossible to try digging and many a time he shifted a fox which others couldn't dislodge.

The song about the terriers was found with old newspaper articles given me by Pearl Wilson, Willie Irving's younger daughter, and the fact that he kept this may well be an indication that Willie had some connection with Turk of Bridekirk, or at least that the Melbreak Hunt did. Turk would have been extensively used as a stud dog, probably with some of the Melbreak terriers and produced offspring which worked at this hunt, and probably other Lakeland packs too. Turk had quickly established himself as one of the best terriers working with a northern pack, or any other pack for that matter.

Sir Wilfred Lawson, Master of the Cumberland Hunt, was

David Davies' foxhounds, bred out of Boaster and Ullswater Melody (c.1920).

out again, this time in the early part of 1935, when they met at Brayton. Hounds were cast off at Brayton Park and a fox broke covert from a grand little spot adjoining the lake. Hounds got away on excellent terms and Reynard tried his best to keep to as much cover as possible, which enabled him to keep ahead of the fast oncoming pack.

He took them into allotments at Harriston and then ran behind the houses, making for the railway and running the line for some distance. He then swam the River Ellen and hounds followed, but scent was extremely difficult when they emerged on the other side, with the result that they slowly followed a fading line to Arkleby Mill where scent now, unfortunately, completely disappeared.

And so to Scaleghyll where hounds had a second fox away which proved to be of the 'straight-necked' (running fast in a straight line) variety. Reynard sped off in the direction of Blaithwaite, but turned before reaching this spot for Black Rigg covert. He crossed the Carlisle road, now running along the railway for Langrigg and the Hall. He stopped short of here, however, and made out for Housenrigg and into Carr Wood. Hounds pressed their fox hard and forced it out of the woods, towards Westnewton village, whereupon he doubled back sharply to the left and came in behind Aspatria Church, where hounds suffered a check (temporary loss of scent).

The Huntsman cast them with an expert eye (this is to direct the hounds to a likely place for them to pick up the trail again, and requires great skill) and sure enough they quickly hit off again and fairly flew now on an improving scent to Westnewton Quarry, where Reynard remained above ground and sped to Carr Wood again.

He left in a hurry as hounds rattled him around this covert and so now he headed for Brayton Park to the Fletchertown road and away for Lees Rigg, where this game fox finally yielded his brush after a fast, exciting hunt in favourable conditions, though the weather had been terrible around that time and a good day was not expected.

The Cumberland Hunt enjoyed some of the best hunting under Sir Wilfred Lawson's Mastership but there were also some very difficult times and in 1936 they had a run of disappointment which meant that kills were few and far between. One of these days was a meet at Whitefield Cottage in early November, quite a remote spot, and the weather was terrible. Apart from the hunt staff, only Sir Wilfred and C.F. Jackson turned out and this was put down to both the isolation of the meet, and the awful weather conditions.

However, a grand fox was soon unkennelled at Ponds Wood and gave hounds a good hunt, despite the conditions. But then scent faded badly and the pack was run off at Mealsgate. Not a 'chump' after that (Cumbrian parlance for 'no find') and so hounds returned to kennels. The next meet was at Dovenby Mill and a large field of 35 riders turned out, but again hounds failed to kill. Reynard left Dovenby Gorse, a place of almost certain finds, and he crossed the Derwent River, making out for the Higham Coverts which have witnessed many a good Melbreak hunt over the years. A number of foxes were roused from this spot, however, and so what was a good hunt was quickly ruined as the pack split in all directions and their original quarry made good his escape.

Hunting in any part of the country isn't easy and the odds are always in Reynard's favour, but hunting in the Lake District, when one considers the challenging landscape and the vast earths available to a hunted fox – earths, by the way, that are impossible to 'stop' – it is incredibly difficult.

A hard dig for fox and terrier with the Lunesdale foxhounds.

In the Lake District, many earths are in fact massive rock-piles, known locally as borrans, with countless exits, so stopping them all up except just one exit for the fox, is just not an option. So it is amazing how many foxes the fell packs killed in an average season.

In the early days, when hounds had quite a bit of harrier blood infused in them to steady them and make them more able to stick to a drag or to keep on to the hunted fox over difficult ground, the hunting was slower and kills fewer. But in more recent decades, particularly after the Second World War, kills steadily climbed to an average of about seventy per season, with some exceptional seasons producing over eighty successful conclusions. This meant good, effective control of fox populations throughout the fells, despite the difficulties of hunting in such country and the cunning of the fell foxes.

A cunning fox for the Blencathra

A day with the Blencathra demonstrated just how cunning foxes could be when hounds were hunting the Skiddaw range in December 1937. This was the holiday season and Huntsman Jim Dalton was known for, in his words, finding the crowds 'far ower noisy'. It was written in a newspaper article, in the mid-1930s after he had retired from the Blencathra, that Jim Dalton had a "steady gait" and that he had "one speed, up hill and down dale, and it was a killer!"

Holiday crowds could get over-excited and loud hollering could spoil hunts and make the hounds unsteady, which Dalton, and to some extent Willie Irving, didn't like. Many a good hunt has been ruined by an inexperienced holiday hunt-follower hollering at a time when hounds should be left to do their job. Hounds spent all this December day on Skiddaw and they drew for quite some distance, crossing at least three ghylls, before several foxes were on foot from woodland clinging to the steep fellside.

Hounds eventually settled on the line of just one fox and Reynard proved a 'game-un'. He was strong indeed and took them at a fast pace all the way to Skiddaw Forest on the other side of this massive mountain range and turned him in by Applethwaite Ghyll, where they killed after a long run. George Bell then cast in the Braithwaite district and another fox soon showed its heels, which took off down the valley and went to ground at Newland Eel Crags, getting himself into a steep gryke (crevass) among the rocks, right in the face of the crag.

This was an incredibly difficult place to work, but a terrier managed to get itself in and it proved a game tyke indeed, as it quickly had its foe by the throat and was intent on throttling it. The Blencathra terrier bloodlines were laced at this time with early pedigree Lakeland terrier blood and the resultant strain was game indeed, famed for being able to kill foxes intent on remaining below ground.

A follower (very likely Douglas Paisley, who carried out much of the terrier work for the Blencathra for a number of decades) managed to get into this rocky spot after a bit of work and fox and terrier were soon 'drawn'. One of Paisley's best during the 1930s was a wheaten-coloured bitch called Trinkett who was famous not only for her grand working qualities, but also for her winning ways at shows where she had picked up several gold medals for best working bitch, just as Irving's Turk picked up several gold medals for best working dog. Trinkett may well have been used on this occasion.

The terrier released its grip and the limp body of the fox was handed to the Huntsman, who placed it on a nearby rock-ledge whilst they sorted themselves out.

However, to the great surprise of all, the fox leapt from the ledge and raced off down the screes in a brave attempt at escape.

Hounds were quickly in action though, and rolled him over before he had run three hundred yards. He was a brave fox, but the tussle with the terrier had been too much. Foxes are well known for faking death, especially in situations where they know they have lost the advantage. They simply go limp and to all intents and purposes look stone dead, but all of a sudden spring to life again.

Terriers will sometimes release their hold on a limp fox thinking the battle is won, and that is when Charlie makes a bid for freedom. Some have succeeded, though, as in this case, a fight with a game terrier just takes too much out of them and usually they do not get far before hounds catch up with them again.

One of the best days the Blencathra ever had was again amongst the massive bulk of the looming Skiddaw mountain range and this was during Jim Dalton's time as Huntsman, one of the most proficient of fell pack hunt servants.

This particular day is celebrated in song and I think it best to include the song, rather than describe the hunting, which was surely one of the best days to ever have occurred in the fells, or, indeed, anywhere else.

The meet was at Sharp Yeat one February morning, probably late in Dalton's career, probably about the mid-1920s. The song is entitled *Sharp Yeat*, or *Five Foxes in One Day*, and goes as follows:

Come, all ye jovial hunters and join me in song,
To sing the praise of a Huntsman bold,
     amidst the cheerful throng.
Jim Dalton's name will live in fame, his gallant hounds so true,
You cannot find their equal if you searched
     the whole world through.

I pray you give attention to what I'm goin' to say,
And I will tell you where he killed five foxes, in just one day.
You foxes must be careful, he still is to the fore,
For sixteen hundred he has killed, and still he is after more.

One February morning, it was Sharp Yeat at nine,
His gallant hounds on Orthwaite Fell, they quickly dragged a line.
They went right out to Cockups, where bold Reynard they espied,
And keeping him in full view, over Burn Dodd they swift-hied.

O'er frozen fell these speedy hounds were gaining on him still,
He found he had a stiffish task to get through Wylie Ghyll.
Down Whiter's he descended, just like a lightning flash,
But those gallant hounds outstripped him
     and killed him in the dash.

A second fox from Dead Crags did slowly steal away,
And med his way to Skiddaw Heights, for there he meant to stay.
Blencathra Pack were on his track he found to his dismay,
And vowed that they would spill his blood, so Reynard made away.

Through Gibraltar he first took those gallant hounds to test,
When climbing to the tops again those hounds did try their best.
They vowed that he should no more feed on Lord Leconfield's grouse,
They ran to view and pulled him down, just behind Skiddaw House.

A third fox went from Lonscale Crag for Skiddaw straight away,
But Rainbow quickly taught him that with her he could not stay.
He had no rest through Skiddaw Breast, then down the Sawmill Ghyll,
They then drove him on to Mirehouse, there to effect a kill.

The snowflakes they were flying, a gale commenced to blow,
Those hunters out on Skiddaw Top were forced to fall in below.
Those hounds of fame, still they were game,
                              and once more they did try,
Two foxes up, the pack they split and away they went in full cry.

Now number four was feeling sore, when an hour or more he'd run,
For Applethwaite he made away, as oft of yore he'd done.
He could not shake them from the trail no matter how he tried,
His time had come, he'd to submit, and, like the others, died.

The valleys around did resound with notes so sweet to hear,
Tired hunters love to hear those notes, their weary hearts to cheer.
There was Roamer, Lonely, Rainbow, Record and Ringlet too,
Those hounds by name I mention, as no one their equal knew.

Down Barkbethdale, straight to the school,
                              bold Reynard made his way,
The children, they joined in the chase, for they were out at play.
They pressed him hard, into the yard,
                              where he some shelter found,
But Roamer was in and dragged him out and slew him on the ground.

From Bassenthwaite the hunters, that day they were but few,
But three there were from Hartcliffe
                              and from Fellside there were two.
Joe Nicholson was absent, Joe Williamson as well,
Bill Todhunter, he does not like to hunt on Orthwaite Fell.

Those Batchelors three, they ought to be the foremost in the chase,
Or take the hint and make a sprint in the matrimonial race.
Foxhunters true are rather few, so do not hesitate,
But keep the hunting families up, before you are too late.

This is a wonderfully evocative song that commemorates what must be one of the greatest of all hunting days to have occurred in the fell country, in severe winter conditions, though scent was obviously very good indeed.

Dalton was a great Huntsman who turned out his hounds in top condition and enjoyed great success as a result. He was also a superb breeder of game terriers and he was one of the first to begin breeding the 'new' strains of what became known as Lakeland terriers. Jim Dalton hunted the famed Blencathra pack from 1894–1930. His memory was so revered that many of the older farmers of the Blencathra country still have his photograph on their walls and even today pictures of Jim Dalton and his hounds and terriers can be found on the walls of many Lake District inns and hotels.

Lake District foxes

The Lake District fox is a hardy beast and the many long runs enjoyed by all of the different packs testifies to this. Not all runs, however, were long and some foxes were less game than others. The Coniston Foxhounds under Ernie Parker were in the Kirkstone district one day in the winter of 1937.

Two foxes were roused on Red Screes above the Kirkstone Pass and hounds typically split. One lot drove their fox down the pass to Hartsop, then back up again, and he was rolled over in the open on the Ullswater side in full view of the car followers. The other lot forced their fox at a rattling pace towards Scandale, through by Dove Crag and on to High Pike. Reynard went to

The dramatic and bleak Honister Crag, scene of many Melbreak and Blencathra hunts, and where a number of hounds have fallen to their deaths.

earth here, but bolted from the bield soon after hounds began marking (baying and scratching where the fox entered), without the need for terriers being entered (put below ground). Hounds got a good start on him and pressed him hard through the Scandale Valley.

The gallant pack, their music echoing around the steep glen, tore after him across the rough fell-sides, but he just managed to get to ground in a borran in Brock Crag before they could catch him. He had been so hard pressed, in fact, that he was unwilling to take his chances in the open again and thus refused to bolt from the eager terriers, who worried him among the vast piles of fallen rock.

One of the longest hunts was when the Cumberland Hunt roused a fox at Torpenhow in the early 1930s, around January time, which went for the Caldbeck Fells, taking hounds well away from the field at a rattling pace that left hunt followers behind. Hounds, in fact, were last seen, or, rather, heard, going like the clappers over the bleak Snow Hill and away into the far distance. It was some time later that reports told of the Blencathra pack joining forces with the Cumberland hounds about Mungrisedale and in this area the combined packs succeeded in killing this game and valiant fox.

Foxes show their cunning in many ways and one of them is by making to ground in earths where terriers just cannot reach them. Foxes know of all these places in their territory and often head straight for them and that is why fell hunting folk have traditionally had certain borrans guarded by hunting enthusiasts who did their utmost to prevent Reynard from going to ground. They very often succeeded, though there have been several occasions when Charlie could not be thwarted. One such occasion was the Melbreak Foxhounds meet at Croasdale in early October 1939, hospitality being shown once again by Mr and Mrs Spedding who regularly welcomed hounds, hunt staff and followers. Hounds were hunting the area for the week and the hunting proved to be both exciting and dramatic.

The first meet saw a fox being roused at Bowness, above Ennerdale Water, and he took hounds above Smithy Beck and on to Scaw, where Reynard earthed in Rowan Tree Bield. Willie Irving put in a brace of his Lakeland terriers, early pedigree stock, and they quickly bolted two foxes. However, Irving managed to get his hounds back on the original hunted fox and he now took them at a really fast pace for Bowness, where the fox 'binked' (leapt for safety) on a crag-ledge.

Hounds soon shifted him, but he binked again above Hollow Ghyll, then went to ground once more on the rough breast of this fell. Terriers quickly bolted him and hounds then pressed him hard until, yet again, he binked in a crag face.

Mischief managed to negotiate this narrow ledge and grabbed his fox, with a fight ensuing that could have seen both hound and fox tumble over the edge to certain death. Charlie did indeed lose his footing, but Mischief just steadied himself in time. Surprisingly, Reynard survived the fall, but hounds soon circled round the back of the crag and at last accounted for their quarry among the screes of Bowness.

On the Saturday hounds were loosed at Croasdale Ghyll and a cold drag was immediately struck, which took them for Tarn Crags, where Charlie was at last afoot. He headed straight for the Scaw and could not be kept out of this safe haven – he knew there he was beyond the attentions of even the gamest of working terriers. Many terriers had failed to reach foxes in this rocky lair and so Willie decided to move on and cut his losses. The day, however, was now warm and dry and scent non-existent, so much drawing of the fells in that area proved fruitless and hounds were taken back to kennels.

There are many impossible places in the Lake District where foxes manage to keep out of reach of terriers, or where a lair is deemed too dangerous to enter a terrier simply because of the number of earth dogs that have been lost there. Any working quarry in the fell country contains impossible places, but especially the Kirkstone quarries.

Broad Howe borran is another bad spot, though several terriers have succeeded in working out Reynard from this place over the decades. Anthony Chapman's Crab, for instance, once bolted a fox from this spot and Eddie Pool of Patterdale, who was present, was so impressed that he brought Crab into his own terrier strain, terriers which saw much service with the Ullswater Foxhounds. George Chapman's Jummy and Mop were other incredibly useful terriers who succeeded in bolting foxes from the fearsome and formidable Broad Howe Borran. Brunt Bield at Buttermere is another notorious place, as is the Brossen Rock of Kirkstone.

Terriers have been known to succeed here at times, though at others foxes just cannot be got at. Dow Crag on Coniston Old Man, Buckbarrow in the Sleddale district, Park Quarries at Troutbeck and Hawkriggs above Leverswater are yet more places where terriers have come to grief whilst trying to bolt foxes. Regular followers of the fell packs know all the dangerous shelves and borrans.

Scent is often difficult in rough country and so deep-scenting hounds are essential, hence the reason for so much harrier blood in the nineteenth and early part of the twentieth centuries. Running dog blood gave fellhounds the necessary speed for catching foxes, but when more emphasis came to be put on good hound work, rather than killing as quickly as possible, hounds' noses needed to be improved and harrier blood produced offspring that still had some speed, but their scenting abilities were greatly improved.

Scent could then be held even across scree, on wall tops and roads. English Foxhound blood from some Shire packs was also used to improve bone and over the years Northumberland's College Valley Foxhound blood has also played a part in providing an outcross for a few of the fell packs, though the College Valley have some fellhound blood running in their veins. From such crosses comes the modern fellhound which, if anything, is possibly faster than its ancestors, though the deep scenting qualities have been retained.

A sunless day with cold but not freezing temperatures was said to be the best for good scent, though scent is unpredictable and with the fox itself being the best judge. If Reynard is in no hurry and keeps just ahead of hounds for much of the time, then it is because he knows that scent is poor. If Charlie puts plenty of distance between himself and his pursuers, more or less from the start, then one can be sure that it is because the fox realises that scent is good, if not 'rattling'.

Much emphasis was put on giving foxes a sporting chance in the Shires, after being bolted by a terrier, but in the fell district little head start or 'law' was offered, as fox hunting was about controlling an agricultural pest, not providing people with 'sport'. Hence although many hunt reports state that a fox was bolted, or dug out and set on its feet again, it rarely got far before being bowled over by hounds.

Some did escape though, despite little 'law' being given, usually because a storm broke suddenly and spoiled scent. There is nothing like a good, heavy downpour for ruining what was formerly a good line.

Effective fox control

The effectiveness of a fell pack in controlling fox numbers has been demonstrated many times throughout several successive generations, and a week with the Blencathra in early December 1934 was just one of these occasions. On one of their more notable days, a fox was quickly roused from Walla Crag near Keswick, which overlooks the beautiful Derwent Water, and it took them right along the face of this range of fells, with the glorious swelling chorus of the hounds resounding from the many crags and woodlands of this rough area, and the sound was heard in Keswick town itself.

The pack crossed screes, the bare woodland floor and the soft springy turf of the open fell-side. Reynard kept to the woods as long as he dared, but was soon heading for the open fell, which he crossed and then dropped into yet more woodland above Thirlmere, after climbing the towering Raven Crag where he attempted to throw hounds off with several 'binks' in this area. He then made through woods in the direction of Armboth and, in desperation, took to a difficult crag ledge.

George Bell was soon up with his pack and he cracked his whip several times before, at last, Charlie shifted and headed down the fell, making out by the foot of the crag. Hounds were quickly on the line again and their musical bay echoed amongst the crags and deep ravines. Charlie then crossed to the Benn side of Thirlmere and was finally caught and killed on the road near Thirlmere Embankment.

Gate Crag then yielded up two more foxes, which caused the Blencathra pack to split. Hounds took one fox down towards Armboth and killed it after a rattling hunt, while the second binked in Worm Crag. Two chaps skilled in working on crags climbed out to him, however, quickly sending him on his way again and the hunt at last resumed, with Charlie taking them over the Rigg to picturesque St John's-in-the-Vale. He crossed by Lowthwaite and climbed the face of Wanthwaite Crag, with hounds doing their best to make progress in this extremely rough and dangerous ground. Their fox then headed for the ridge of mighty Helvellyn, Great Dodd and Brown Crag, before making for low country where he was finally run into at Fisher Place.

During another meet that week, a brace of fox were accounted for on the Bassenthwaite side of Skiddaw and a sixth fox, hunted about the Threlkeld countryside, was driven into a wet peat earth and terriers were put in. Albert Benson was Whipper-in at this time and his famous terrier Red Ike was working with the Blencathra pack. Maybe one of the terriers was Ike, who now went in and succeeded in bolting the fox after a little 'persuasion'. Reynard was rather 'clagged-up' with wet peat from the earth and was freezing from the icy underground waters and so he didn't get far before hounds finally pulled him down. Six foxes in one week of hunting is proof enough that the fell packs

Johnny Richardson and Ronnie Cape heading out from Grange, Borrowdale – a valley full of dangerous crags.

carried out effective pest control for the Lake District farmers and shepherds.

'Urban' foxes

Foxes in the fells occasionally took to the streets of villages, and sometimes even the towns were also negotiated, with Ambleside and Keswick featuring in some exciting hunts. One such time was when the Blencathra drew for well over two hours before they finally had their fox afoot from Iron Crag in the Thirlmere district. Hounds got away well on their fox, who headed for the formidable borrans at Gate Crag, but one or two of the keener followers stood guard and drove him on.

He now took to the tops and hounds followed across the bleak fells, before dropping down at Walla Crag to Falcon Crag. Charlie then took hounds to Castle Crag, but he was so hard pressed that he made for the outskirts of Keswick and onto the main Keswick-Ambleside road, before taking to the streets of the town. Hounds managed to hold scent, despite the obvious difficulties, and finally pulled their fox down by a wire fence after a long and incredibly exciting hunt. I have no date for this hunt, but it was sometime during the 1930s.

The Eskdale and Ennerdale pack had a very good day in the Egremont district after they had been called in to hunt down foxes that were taking a heavy toll on the townfolk's poultry. Arthur Irving was the Huntsman at this time and so it was probably during the 1940s and took place in the month of November. Hounds dragged out to Linethwaite Woods near Bigrigg and the pack soon had several foxes on the move. Guns had been employed to ensure a kill and at least one was shot by a Mr N. Wilson.

The others, it seems, were taken by hounds and terriers and one was a dog fox weighing 19lbs, which was carried back to kennels by 'Dodger' Pattinson, the keen Melbreak and Eskdale and Ennerdale supporter. Mr Pattinson was a miner who resided at Egremont and walked hounds and terriers for both of these packs. Willie Irving had several hounds and terriers walked with Pattinson, who was one of the keenest of all followers, acting as unpaid Whipper-in at the Eskdale and Ennerdale whenever needed. This hunt was, again, a great demonstration of how useful fell packs were at catching livestock-killing predators.

Another great demonstration of this was at a more recent meet near Mungrisedale when Barry Todhunter had only recently taken over as Huntsman. The meet was at Mines Bridge and many supporters turned out for what proved to be a superb day. Barry loosed his eager pack on the fells and drew back towards Swineside, the hounds immediately feathering amongst deep heather all around, with Charlie getting up in full view of the field only minutes later. This fox, however, had lingered just a little too long and was quickly accounted for, with Careless leading the pack down the fell-side.

A second fox was roused as the pack drew towards Carrock Mines and the deep heather nearly proved its undoing, but rough ground and scree aided its desperate attempt to put some ground between itself and its hunters. Reynard then made good through Swineside Breast and negotiated the incredibly rough going as only foxes can. Charlie proved game and took hounds right out onto the fells, coming by Carrock Pike. Hounds pressed him hard about here and the big rocks on Carrock gave him a temporary respite, but hounds kept to their task with hardly a check and eventually forced him to 'bink' at a dangerous crag. Hounds bravely negotiated this tricky place and went on to catch a fine dog fox.

Two more foxes were roused a little later, at Penn End, and, as usual, hounds split. The main lot took their fox out by Carrock Pike, then dropped at Rake Trod. They now pressed

John Dixon waits for a bolt with the Lunesdale hounds. Borrans like this are common at the foot of crags.

him hard and forced him to go to ground in a large borran on Carrock front. This rock earth proved deep and difficult, but the carefully-bred Blencathra terriers soon found their fox skulking among the huge mass of stone piles and they eventually succeeded in bolting their quarry, which weaved through the massive boulders strewn across this area, but he was pulled down close to the road shortly afterwards. All of the pack were now back as one, as the other fox had been hunted over to Driggeth Mines area and was finally caught in lowland. A spectacular day drew to a close (bad weather had set in, or even more foxes may have been taken that day), with four foxes hunted and four foxes accounted for, all across incredibly rough ground.

7

HUNTING THE HARE

Up to the 1800s, hare hunting with hounds had been far more popular than fox hunting in those parts of Cumberland, Westmorland and North Lancashire that now come under the one county of Cumbria. Any means were used to catch and kill foxes, including the use of bobbery packs made up of all kinds of dogs, including hounds and street curs, as well as guns. These mixed dogs lived with their owners all over the district, but at the call of the hunter's horn, they would be released to join the pack, or go with their owners, and a scratch pack would assemble.

But hares were treated as a more sacred animal, to be hunted with organised packs that, in the main, were trencher-fed. A few packs were kennelled, but these mostly belonged to well-off gentry, rather than farmers and other Dalesfolk. Hunting the fox didn't really suit many dalesfolk during the eighteenth and early part of the nineteenth centuries due to the long distances needed to be covered before mechanised transport, whereas hares found much more favour as quarry.

With the hares, who ran shorter distances and always moved in a large circular trail, great hound work was enjoyed at close quarters – any follower of beagles or harriers will tell you that their hunting is far more visible than trying to watch foxhounds at work in which the pack often went out of sight for long periods of time.

Yew Crags at Honister, an exhausting and testing place to chase a hare.

The fields of the lower dales in those days, even up to the Second World War, were mainly used for crop growing and so hunting the hare was considered necessary, though they were also hunted for the great hound work that could be enjoyed, as well as the social side of life that came with it. The Lakeland valleys can be dreary places in winter and hunting helped folk get through the bleak months, providing a great social basis for keeping in touch with friends and neighbours.

The hounds after hares were deep-scenting and dwelt on a line for hours at a time in some cases, but often remaining in the same valley throughout the entire hunt and thus providing good spectator sport too. With fox hunting, one could end up several valleys away from home, facing a long trudge back, often in darkness. Hares provided a great and not too exhausting day out for farmers and dalesfolk.

Hunting the fox in those days usually meant a start at daybreak, or very soon afterwards, in order to take up the drag until Reynard was finally located and flushed from his daytime retreat. But hares were found above ground at any time of day, so meets could be arranged for any hour starting even as late as lunchtime. This was very convenient for farmers in particular, who could get their milking and other tasks done before going hunting.

Large numbers of hares were not taken during any average season, though on days when scent was very good, hounds have been known to account for as many as two or three in one day. Then, just as with fox hunting, celebrations were often held after a hunt, or the night before hunting was to take place.

Hares can be as cunning as foxes, and are worthy of a good pack of hounds. Most kept to the low country and remained in the valley but those that did take to the mountains were often the ones that succeeded in escaping. In fact, some hares preferred to live on mountainsides and the tops of lower fells, shunning the low country, and these mountain hares gave hounds good runs. Hares are plentiful in the Lake District today, but during the times when crops grew in every valley, they were far more numerous and that is why several packs, dozens of them at one time, were found throughout the fells, with some small towns and villages having more than one pack kennelled in the vicinity.

Ambleside housed as many as three packs, though not all hunted hares. Foxhound and Otterhound packs were also common, with deer being the principal quarry of one or two.

Windermere harriers

One of the best hare packs was the Windermere Harriers and their glory days were those when Anthony Chapman, the father of George Chapman who took over the Coniston Foxhounds in 1908 and quickly shaped them into a first-rate fox killing pack, hunted these hounds. Anthony Chapman had unimaginable powers of endurance and was an expert houndsman to boot, so the Windermere Harriers under his Huntsmanship became incredibly useful and much of their hunting was carried out in much the same country that the Coniston Foxhounds still cover to this day, with several hunts taking to the mountains.

These harriers also hunted foxes and marts (pinemartens, or polecats) whenever one could be found and so Anthony Chapman also kept one or two game terriers and he bred some incredibly useful stock that saw service with both his pack and the Coniston Foxhounds. It is difficult to ascertain exactly which terriers belonged to George Chapman and which belonged to his father, Anthony.

The reformed Windermere Harriers were later hunted by Albert Benson, one-time Whipper-in to the Blencathra during the 1930s, when John Bulman was Master, then by Anthony Barker of Patterdale who enjoyed great success with this pack, ably assisted by his daughters, Diane and Heather. Anthony Barker also roused foxes with this pack and some long hunts ensued, though hares were officially the only quarry they sought. This pack, sadly, no longer exists.

John Bulman took over the Windermere Harriers, becoming Master and Huntsman in 1956 and soon established himself as one of the keenest Huntsmen to field a pack of hounds. He had been born at Eskdale, but moved to the Langdales as a young boy when his parents took over the Dungeon Ghyll Hotel.

John took to farming and was noted for breeding good quality shorthorn cattle, which were once very popular throughout the country. However, hunting was his real passion and he followed both the Eskdale and Ennerdale and Coniston Foxhounds,

John Bulman leads the Windermere Harriers.

whilst hares were hunted with the Windermere pack. He also became Joint-Master of the Ullswater pack from 1970-75. John was a great friend of that famous terrier breeder Frank Buck when Buck was hunting the Wensleydale Harriers for Donald Sinclair (Seigfreid Farnon of James Herriot's wonderful books). Buck received generous donations of fallen stock from the Dales farmers, and Bulman would travel over to Harmby, a small village only a stone's-throw away from Leyburn, in order to pick up regular supplies of surplus feed that Buck's hounds couldn't manage to get through. Those were great hunting days and both Buck and Bulman enjoyed great success with their Harriers.

Today's beagle packs

Today the four main packs that hunt in and around Cumbria are the Vale of Lune Harriers, the Blackcombe Beagles, the Cumbria Beagles and the Bleasdale Beagles, though other packs still visit the area each season (and nowadays either trail, or rabbit, is the official quarry).

The Colne Valley used to visit the Melbreak country each season and they provided some wonderful hunting in this area, with one of the best spots being on the lower fell-sides along the Loweswater-Lamplugh road where great views can be enjoyed of hounds working. Willie Irving often hunted with this pack, as did De Courcy Parry's (Dalesman) hounds, which at one time were known as the Troutbeck Lodge Hounds. Many a good hare hunt has been enjoyed in the Melbreak country and Anthony Barker used to take his harriers there by invitation of the Melbreak Hunt.

One of the most beautiful of hunting areas is that covered by the Vale of Lune which is found in both North Lancashire and in Cumbria. One of their best seasons was in 1926-1927 when they enjoyed 43 days in the field, with 5 days lost to bad weather and sickness, and 23 hares were accounted for. Only two days proved blank, ie didn't even put up a hare, that season.

In early March of 1927 hounds met at Melling and a large field turned out for what was the last day of that season. Maher took his hounds and drew several places, including Cockshotts, Lodge House Farm and Bainspark, without finding. He then cast at Spinks Ghyll and here a hare was at last on its legs. Puss took them towards Melling and to Lodge Farm, back past Spinks Ghyll and across the Hornby-Melling road and away for Taylors Holme. Their hare then re-crossed the road and went over the tops to Park House Farm and on into Hornby Castle Big Wood, where the glorious swell of hound music echoed and re-echoed amongst the tall trees. She then ran hounds round and round these plantations and refused to leave. Her scent soon became so confusing that in the end she was given best (left alone) and a good season came to a natural end with the close season just about to begin.

A few days before this, hounds had met at Redwell and Huntsman Maher quickly had a hare afoot from the corner of a field close to where hounds had just met. Puss went by Swarthdale in the direction of Kellet and on past Kirk House Farm and Kirkland Barrow, with hounds speaking gloriously to a good line. She then turned and headed all the way back to where she had been found earlier, possibly in order to shake hounds and a fresh hare got up here and took the pack away from her – a cunning move!

Hounds surged 'forrard' on a fresh line and Maher knew they had changed quarry by the upturn in their beautiful music and a quickened pace.

Their fresh quarry crossed the road near Redwell, past the gamekeeper's cottage, on through Capernway Wood and across the Borwick road for Cragg Lots. Leaving here some time later, she now made her way past Gunnerlodge Gate and Borwick Station before re-crossing the Borwick road. Puss now ran parallel to the railway line all the way to the Viaducts, where hounds were finally stopped after a good hunt of 45-minutes on this fresh hare alone. The ground covered was quite extensive, which says much about the very fast pace hounds ran that day.

In November 1933 the Furness and District Beagles met at Greenhurst, Cartmel. Hounds were loosed at Barnsley Lot and a hare soon started up on the higher ground here. The pack of beagles came together rather smartly and set off in fine style on a good fell hare. Puss now led them downhill, past the little pond and into Seatle Big Wood, where hounds bustled her around this covert for quite some time, the fast-paced little pack keeping the pressure up as they followed her keen line.

The hare then broke cover at the top end of this wood, right in front of hounds, and ran parallel with the high wall, until reaching the Cartmel road. She cunningly made as much use of the road as possible and succeeded, in the end, in throwing off her eager pursuers, which, despite their best efforts and assistance from their Huntsman, just couldn't stick to her tracks.

They next drew School Lot and a drag was hit off almost immediately. Hounds persevered on a catchy bit of drag and they soon had their reward when a hare was up ahead of them. This hare was another cunning adversary and she took them to high ground where she made full use of the still-dense bracken beds, standing out starkly in glorious russet against the rough ground of the fells, all the way to Speetbank.

Here they swung left-handed and dropped into the valley, disappearing into thick coverts here. Hounds eventually pushed her out of profuse undergrowth and she now took them for high ground again, climbing out the other side of the valley until reaching Howbarrow, where, after much hard and gallant work, hounds lost her.

No hares accounted for but hunt staff and followers had enjoyed great hound work.

There are several differences between hunting the fox and hunting the hare. Foxes, for instance, will generally leave covert rather sharpish and keep well ahead of the pack, seeking to put as much distance between themselves and their pursuers as possible, especially if scent is good.

Hares, on the other hand, will often allow hounds to work right up to them before putting on a burst of speed for some distance and then 'sitting' again at some chosen 'form' (hollow in the ground) only making a move when hounds get close again. This can go on for a long time and distance and hares usually take hounds in large circles.

Foxes sometimes go in circles too, though not nearly as often as hares. Hares, like foxes, will use cunning in order to attempt

Jim Dalton with Blencathra hounds in Borrowdale (c.1925).

Tommy Dobson (left) and Willie Porter at a huge borran.

to throw hounds and running over their old line is just one ploy that makes hunting them so difficult. Roads, sheep and cattle are also deliberately used by the hare to foil the line.

One of the cleverest tricks, however, is the one used when 'puss' simply disappears and cannot be found again, no matter how much Huntsman and hounds search. Foxes sometimes do this, though usually after a sudden storm has ruined scent, or after a fox has been 'headed' when almost running into one of the followers, but not nearly as often as hares mysteriously vanish into thin air, taking their scent with them.

Hares, though, are generally easier to find than foxes and, as stated earlier, usually remain in a limited area. Some long runs, however, have occurred over the years and one of the best was with the Vale of Lune Harriers in November 1933.

Hounds met at Dent's Bridge, Casterton, only a stone's throw from Kirkby Lonsdale, on a cold, wet morning that proved one of the best for holding scent. A hare was found on Casterton Fell and this took hounds all over the hills and pastures of this area before finally being accounted for after a long and gruelling three hours in terrible weather.

The next November meet was at the *Sportsman's Inn*, Hutton Roof and a hare was quickly found just below the inn. She gave a rattling fifteen-minute run before being pulled down on the crag. A second hare was then roused from a Mr Burrow's meadow and took hounds quickly to Mackereth's Intake and back left-handed to the gamekeeper's cottage. Puss then took to the woods and the music of hounds was at its grandest as it echoed amongst the tall trees and kept followers in touch as they went out to High Biggins. Hounds pushed her hard about here and finally pulled her down in Biggins Grounds after a superb 50-minutes of great hound work, carried out at a fast pace – very fast at times.

Yet another hare was roused by this eager pack, from Mackereth's Intake, and she took off in the direction of the *Sportsman's Inn* and gave hounds a run that took in two circles before finally being run out of scent after she had reached Spittle Wood.

The next meet was at Farleton and hounds soon found on Mr Wilkinson's Lots. Their hare raced away and took them at a fast pace to Jacky Wood and after two circular runs was finally lost in Engine Wood.

A second hare was roused from Mashiter's Holme and she proved a 'game un'. Puss ran three good circuits by Rodgerson's Holme, Kitchen's Meadow and back to where found. She then took to shingle beds by the river Lune and here succeeded in shaking off her eager seekers, who just couldn't hold her line any longer. No matter though, for their hare had given them a good hour and a half of fine hunting and all were well satisfied with their day among some of the most beautiful scenery this country has to offer.

Hunting the hare was another good way of enjoying both great exercise and a good social life and it is satisfying to report that beagle and harrier packs up and down the country, not just in Cumbria, have managed to keep going after the hunting ban. Social occasions continue to be part and parcel of modern restricted hunting. Good hound breeding also continues and in Cumbria some of the most hard working and persevering of hare hunting hounds have been bred. They have to have such qualities, due to the rough nature of the terrain, which can vary from pasture to rough fell, to scree, to road, to woodland, and all within the space of a few hundred yards. Such conditions will greatly test the abilities of any type of hound, no matter what the quarry hunted.

West Cumberland beagles

The West Cumberland Beagles were yet another pack that hunted the fell country and they enjoyed a particularly outstanding week during the 1940s. The beagles were loosed from Mr Nicholson's farm at Netherstainton and they quickly roused a hare and killed it. A second hare gave a good run for upwards of two hours and eventually made good her escape by taking to the main road. The Huntsman then called hounds off, as traffic was quite heavy and the danger to hounds was obvious.

On another occasion, hounds met at Fauld Gate and soon had a good fell hare on the move, which proved quite a cunning beast. She kept taking to the roads and succeeded in making things very difficult for hounds, until a fresh hare got up and led hounds away from her.

This fresh hare raced away and made out right over the high tops, with hounds getting away from their Huntsman and followers and disappearing into the fells for about an hour. Puss eventually brought them back full circle, but it was now getting

Robin Logan of the Coniston foxhounds.

late and hounds were reluctantly called off. However, events took an unusual turn in that, as they were making back to the meet, the unlucky original hare got up right in front of hounds and was quickly caught.

The final hunt that week proved a wash-out, as heavy rain came on just as they were about to start and so hunting had to be abandoned.

Caldbeck beagles

'Mowdy' Robinson of Hollins Farm, Lorton Vale, invited the Caldbeck Beagles to spend a day in the Melbreak country, where mountain hares were numerous. Several were astir as hounds drew the steep hillsides and lower pastures and one hare was accounted for in Dodd Bottom, close to the Melbreak kennels,

The terrain has insurmountable crags, for both foxes and hounds.

with Willie Irving's youngest daughter, Pearl, being one of the first to be in at the kill. Jerry Robinson, a brother of 'Mowdy' Robinson, was holidaying in the Lakes at the time and enjoyed a great day out with the beagles.

He had left the fell country many years earlier in order to hunt a Midland pack of otterhounds, but was by this time (late 1940s) in retirement. These were the sons of old Tom Robinson of Dub Hall, Arlecdon, who was a great ploughman who won many awards at ploughing matches all over the north of England. He was also a champion Cumberland and Westmorland wrestler in his younger days. The Robinson family were stalwart supporters of the Melbreak Foxhounds, especially during Irving's time, though Tom Robinson, the son of Mowdy, was one-time Whipper-in to Harry Hardisty.

Hare hunting has traditionally enjoyed great support in Cumbria and countless fascinating and exciting accounts can be related by those who have regularly followed hounds in this enchanting part of the world.

◇◇◇◇◇◇◇◇◇

8

CRAG-FAST

Today busy roads are the major danger faced by any pack of hounds on the line of a game fox, but in the past, crags were considered the greatest of all hazards. Hounds could either fall from these treacherous ledges, or become crag-fast after following a fox out onto a narrow ledge, or while climbing up or down a crag face following a route taken by the fox.

Crags have always been a favourite haunt of fell foxes who used them as daytime retreats, or when seeking refuge from hound and terrier. When a fox took to a crag while being hunted, this became known as 'binking' (or 'benking') and was a most effective way of escaping the attentions of hounds, though on many occasions hunting folk proved as cunning as their adversaries and managed to flush foxes from these otherwise safe sanctuaries. Sometimes, though, Reynard could not be shifted and hounds would have to move on.

Cracking a whip sometimes flushed a 'binked' fox. If that didn't work, then throwing stones close to where Charlie sat on a ledge on the sheer-drop rock face would occasionally get him moving. And, if such methods failed, then sending out a hound, or even better a terrier, to shift the fox, was sometimes the only option.

On occasion one of the more stout-hearted followers would climb either up, or down, the crag and move the fox on. Hunting in the fells was about predator control and if every fox that took to the crags was left for another day, control would have been

Gordon Stagg, ex-Whipper-in with the Melbreak, holds the reins with Vic, a Lakeland terrier bred by Willie Irving, next to the sheepdog.

ineffectual. Hunting reports, in particular the full and fascinating diaries of the late Willie Irving, clearly demonstrate just how often foxes took to crags and the difficulties Huntsmen often had in getting them to move on.

It was whilst negotiating these narrow ledges in order to flush Reynard into the open again that hounds or terriers, became trapped on the crag ledge, unable to find a way back. Sometimes a hound or terrier and maybe the fox as well, would fall from the crag and plunge to their deaths, though occasionally a hound, terrier or fox, would survive the fall and some even get up and carry on working!

There are quite a number of fell pack accounts of hounds falling a hundred feet or more and then getting to their feet and rejoining the hunt. There are also many accounts of crag-fast hounds and their rescues. One of the most amazing of all accounts was a report concerning the Melbreak Foxhounds when hunting in the Buttermere area in 1936.

This was in springtime so was probably a lambing call, when hounds soon had a fox on the go, which eventually took to a 'bink' at Yew Crag, opposite Honister Quarry. Willie Irving, the Huntsman at that time, was going to leave Charlie for another day, as the place was too dangerous to allow hounds to have a go at moving him.

However, the hunt secretary decided to have a go and carefully climbed down the crag where Reynard had gone under a huge rock and couldn't be reached. The noise our stout-hearted climber made alerted Charlie to imminent danger and he made the fatal error of deciding to quit what would have been a very safe sanctuary.

And so the hunted fox made a move and climbed out on to an even higher part of Yew Crags. One of the hounds, Marksman, had been questing around a buttress of the crag and attempted to make out for where Charlie now resided, but Marksman lost his footing and fell 100 feet. Reynard slipped at almost exactly the same time and he too fell down the crag about 80 feet into a deep gully, turning over and over in the air.

Willie cringed as his beloved hound fell and no-one wished to see a fox die in such a manner either, but, miraculously, both hound and fox seemed barely the worse for their potentially tragic falls and Charlie now came tearing out of the ravine at great speed, with hounds quickly in action and getting themselves onto his line. Amazingly, Marksman soon rejoined the pack too and they now hunted their fox down and across the Honister Pass road with Singwell leading.

The valiant fox crossed the mountain beck and made out for the steep fell-side, but hounds pressed him hard about here

A Lakeland terrier in 1911. This one, owned by a relative of Gary Middleton, worked with the hounds in North Yorkshire.

and finally pulled him down before he had travelled far up the hillside, where he no doubt intended to make for yet more dangerous crags.

It often fell to the Huntsman, Whipper-in, or a keen follower, to carry out a rescue of a crag-fast hound and some of these were bold indeed, requiring very stout hearts. Sometimes, though, hounds do get off the crag safely and this occurred during yet another Melbreak hunt in the 1930s, when Marksman and Singwell were stalwarts of the pack.

Hounds had hunted a fox hard and driven him to the crags at Buxom Hows where he 'binked' on a ledge above a particularly precipitous part of the crag-face. Bugler led out onto the crag and he managed to negotiate the tricky route, finally jumping onto the ledge and making a grab for the fox. Charlie dodged the lunging attack, but lost his footing whilst doing so and fell over 100 feet onto rocks below. Hounds rushed down around the crag, but Reynard had perished from the fall and his lifeless body was left unmolested by the pack. Bugler meanwhile had just managed to keep his footing and, after some tricky work among the rocks, he found a way off the narrow ledge, much to the relief of hunt staff and followers.

However, at the very next meet, hounds were not so fortunate. The Melbreak met at Scale Bridge near Loweswater and a fell fox was soon found at Blea Crag, which climbed out at a very fast pace past Scale Force and on to Red Pike, from where it crossed to High Stile and High Crag. Reynard now descended towards Gamlin End and then began a steep climb onto Haystacks, which was the late author Alfred Wainwright's favourite mountain and the place where his ashes are now scattered.

Charlie now made down the steep and dangerous face of Big Stack and arrived safely at the foot of this place, but one hound, Marksman, after attempting to follow his fox, found himself crag-fast. The rest of the pack managed to get around the crags in one way or another and kept the hunt going to Warnscale, over the forbidding Fleetwith Pike, a bleak, fearsome spot in midwinter and not much more welcoming in summer either, and out by Honister Pass to Grey Knotts.

After circling this mountainous and particularly craggy district, with the thrilling cry of hounds echoing amongst the steep sides of this valley, Charlie re-crossed Honister Pass and took to Honister Crag after gaining much ground on what was now a difficult line.

Hounds had to admit defeat soon after and so Willie collected his pack and made back to where Marksman had got himself into difficulty. He had earlier left Albert Thomas, his Whipper-in, back at the crag with Marksman.

A white Lakeland terrier owned by the Middleton family.

On collecting hounds, Willie discovered that Chancellor and Dauntless were also missing and they too were later found crag-fast. Darkness was now falling fast and the area around Big Stack was considered so dangerous that it was deemed necessary to leave three hounds out on the crag ledge overnight.

One can imagine what a disturbed and restless night Willie and the Melbreak followers must have had, being eager to get their hounds off the crags as quickly as possible, lest one or other weakened and plunged to almost certain death. Fortunately, conditions were mild, so there were no fears that the hounds might freeze to death.

There were plenty of volunteers next morning to help rescue

the hounds, but the dangerous task fell to Whipper-in Albert Thomas and J. Bland of Wasdale. After using ropes to negotiate the steep crags, this pair of stout-hearted fell hunters succeeded in reaching and rescuing all three hounds without mishap, much to the relief of everyone.

The Blencathra were in the Borrowdale Valley some time during the 1930s and they enjoyed a long and hard run of five hours after a game fox that eventually 'binked' in Gate Crag, it had tempted five hounds to try negotiating this tricky place in an attempt to flush him out. However, they were soon crag-fast and couldn't move from their perilous position on a ledge. Unfortunately, Traveller, a very useful Blencathra hound, fell 30 feet from a ledge and injured himself internally. He seemed little worse for wear at the time, but sadly died later that day.

The task of rescuing the other four hounds fell to Whipper-in Albert Benson and he was lowered down the crag on ropes. He succeeded in getting ropes around all four hounds, which were safely lifted off the crag one by one. What courage it took Benson to be lowered down a crag in this fashion and to rescue hounds which otherwise would have to be left until they perished through lack of food and water, or from exposure.

This knack of being lowered down crag faces on ropes is said to have been started by those seeking to work out slate from these vast rocky places, but I wonder if it was first carried out by hunters seeking to rescue their gallant hounds after following a 'binked' fox that stubbornly refused to shift! Whilst this rescue was occurring, their fox made off the crag and the rest of the pack were quickly laid on by Huntsman George Bell. They pushed their quarry hard for some distance and eventually rolled him over near Manesty, over on the western side of Derwentwater.

It is bad enough when tragedy strikes among hounds and terriers, but even worse when humans are involved, such as at the opening meet of the Cumberland Hunt during the 1930s. This traditional meet was held at Isel Hall, the residence of the then-Master Sir Wilfred Lawson. The day was gloriously fine with much keen anticipation for what lay ahead. Sir Wilfred Lawson had taken a tumble at Dalston point to point in April of that year and had been badly injured, but had by this time made a complete recovery. The autumn colours amongst surrounding woodlands were glorious and it was expected that scent would be good and coverts holding.

Hounds soon found a brace of foxes in Blindcrake Ghyll and all got onto the line of just one, racing away for Sunny Brows, where Charlie went to ground and was accounted for by the terrierman (probably Allinson of Cockermouth). Sadly, in the process of this hunt, a young lad with a promising future was very severely injured. John Barwise Kerr of Linskeld Farm came off his horse when it reared and fell on top of him, rolling right over its rider in the process of trying to get up.

Unfortunately, his injuries proved too severe and the poor young lad died some time later that day. It could never have been foreseen that such a glorious hunting morning would turn into a day of such tragedy.

When the Melbreak were hunting in the Buttermere area in April 1942, a bitch hound called Tulip fell fifty feet down a sheer-crag face on Robinson Fell after pressing her fox hard. She ran right over the edge and was badly shaken by her ordeal, losing several teeth in the fall. Amazingly, she went on to make a full recovery and rejoined the pack the very next season.

Sometimes, though, things went well in the roughest of country and hounds got through crags and other nigh-on impossible obstacles without incident. That was the case when the Eskdale and Ennerdale pack were hunting in the Ennerdale district in January 1948, when Art Irving was Huntsman of that famous pack. A single hound, Trinket by name, ran her fox along the fells and pushed it so hard that she forced it to ground on the Scaw. Willie Porter, the long-serving Master of the Eskdale and Ennerdale Foxhounds, wasn't far behind, Art having gone after the rest of the pack who were hunting a second fox. Porter entered his terriers into this rocky lair where they quickly found and bolted Charlie, and Trinket soon ran her quarry down alone and unaided. It was said that she had crossed some of the roughest country in the fells during this hunt and one wonders how on earth she managed to do so without getting herself crag-fast, as had so many others during such gloriously fast hunts.

In more recent years, rescues have become a little more dramatic and during the 1990s several of the Ullswater hounds had had to be airlifted off Black Crag after they had followed their fox onto this notorious spot. In pre-helicopter times though, quarrymen in particular were very handy at rescuing crag-fast hounds, as they were used to being lowered down crag faces on ropes. Rock climbers have also played a major part in helping to rescue hounds from crag ledges, and they have also helped bring out hounds and terriers that have fallen down old mineshafts. Literally hundreds of hound and terrier rescues have taken place throughout the fell country and those who have participated have either been incredibly brave, or downright crazy!

9

HUNTING THE OTTER & THE MART

The Lake District has been a haven for otters and until the 1960s, they were very numerous and known for their fish-killing and so several packs of otterhounds were found in this part of the country. Many packs ceased hunting the otter when it became rare, long before it was officially banned in 1978.

The Kendal and District and the Carlisle and District Otterhounds were the most famous and enduring packs, but there were many others such as the Cockermouth, Egremont, Grasmere, Lake District and West Cumberland Otterhounds. Jack Porter also ran a small private pack of otterhounds during the time that Arthur Irving hunted the Eskdale and Ennerdale pack and he enjoyed some very successful hunts with his small team of hounds and terriers.

Some used traditional heavy-coated and deep scenting otterhounds, while the majority simply used foxhounds out at their summer walks. For instance, Peter Long, who was an Egremont man and a fanatical hunter and terrier breeder who played a large part in producing several of the foundation terriers that formed both the pedigree and unregistered strains of Lakeland terrier, walked hounds for foxhound and beagle packs and hunted these hounds at otter during the summer months.

He also hunted fox, badger, hare and deer with his charges. Long hunted with the Eskdale and Ennerdale pack in the main, though he also followed the Melbreak Foxhounds whenever possible, as did his son, G.H. Long.

Although there were many packs of hounds hunting otter, there were also small terrier packs run at this quarry by some, including Joe Armstrong, Frank and Jack Pepper, and Eddie Pool. Many of the Egremont set used packs of terriers too, though usually alongside a few hounds. Otters were not particularly hard to find in those days, though some of the hunts were arduous and often led into high ground, with otters taking to the fells and the rocky places from which it was sometimes impossible to extricate them.

Terriers were sometimes badly mauled by this hard biting quarry, but it is said that two of champion-breeder Douglas Paisley's pedigree Lakelands once killed a fully-grown otter and, if true, it was no mean feat. Paisley, among others, was a keen otter hunter and the photographs included in this chapter were found in a drawer by Gordon Martin when he and his wife Mary bought the small wooden bungalow with terrific views of the Skiddaw range, where Paisley had spent much of his fascinating life with his famous strain of Lakeland terrier kennelled at the bottom of his large garden.

It seems Paisley took some of these photos himself and on the opposite page you can see the otter bolting from what are probably Paisley's Lakeland terriers still below ground. This wonderfully atmospheric photo, taken in the late 1920s, captures a lost age when some truly great terrier breeders had unlimited freedom to work their earth dogs to a variety of testing quarry.

Visiting otter packs

Although Cumbria had several otter hunting packs of its own, there were also several that visited the area, especially from Wales and Devon, as well as one or two packs from around the Midlands. A visiting pack, the Bucks Otterhounds, came for a week of otter hunting in the summer of 1952 and enjoyed some good days.

One of the best hunts was when hounds drew up the river after a meet at the mouth of the river Ehen. Hounds found an otter after drawing for maybe a mile or more, but it didn't run far before going to ground. These visiting packs often brought a few followers north with them and they always came with a few handy terriers too.

A brace were now put into this holt and they were soon heard to be baying strongly, harassing their otter around the underground lair for the next hour or so, until he at last bolted and went away at rather a fast pace.

Hounds now raced back the way they came and poor scent meant they began to struggle close to an industrial site, though surges of scent on the water suggested their quarry was still in

Coats are slung over the bough as the diggers get to work. This photo captures the dramatic moment when an otter makes a dash for the river.

181

the area and probably skulking below ground once again.

Hounds finally marked under a large rock and strong arms and stout crowbars were employed to try to get things moving again. And they succeeded. The rock was moved a little and the otter bolted immediately, heading towards the sea. Hounds caught their otter close to the beach after a fast hunt. It had been a remarkable hunt on an idyllic summer day amongst some of the most breathtaking riverside scenery in the world.

Hounds drew on upstream until near teatime, but no more otters were found that day.

Another otter hunt began about the lower end of Derwent-water and a small pack of terriers, fielded by Jack and Frank Pepper, soon found and hunted their quarry into the marshy areas all over the lower parts of this valley. Their quarry then took them onto the river and they managed to hunt downstream, past Grange and to the rocky banks below the famous Bowderstone where the Peppers lived, in the old cottage originally built as a guide's residence. I believe it was a tea-room when the Peppers lived there.

The otter now got in among the rocks and Frank entered two of his best terriers, Blossom and Peggy (this Peggy was sold to Willie Irving in the early 1930s and can, I believe, be seen on the far left of the famous Crummock Water photograph on the cover of my book, *Willie Irving, Terrierman, Huntsman and Lakelander* published by Merlin Unwin Books, 2008). These two terriers stayed with their quarry until they were finally dug out from among the rocks (together with the dead otter) after much hard graft, sweat and toil with crowbars.

Otters could cover vast distances and occasionally hounds, or terriers, drowned whilst in pursuit. Otters also got into some very difficult places and some of the harder terriers were badly mauled whilst attempting to evict them. It took a clever, 'stand off and bay' type of terrier to work out an otter without receiving damage to themselves and many of the Lakeland variety of earth dog were just too hard for such quarry, though some, like Douglas Paisley and Willie Irving, did use their stock at otter.

Willie would always try to avoid his bolder terriers getting

On the trail of an otter which has sensibly sought refuge in the reeds.

a mauling, however, and preferred to use his more cunning and cautious charges against otters.

Many of these Lakeland terriers killed foxes, rather than bolted them, as Irving's diaries clearly show, but some were clever enough to tackle badgers and otters without too much injury to themselves. Peggy, for instance, the bitch with the Peppers in the Borrowdale Valley photograph, was one such Lakeland who would kill a reluctant fox, yet she proved very handy for badger digging and bolting otters. Many Lakelands, in fact, proved incredibly useful otter dogs and several of the fell pack Huntsmen, Willie Irving and Jim Dalton included, loaned their terriers to otter hunting packs during the summer months.

One of the most successful Huntsmen of an otterhound pack was William Sanderson, who became Huntsman of the Carlisle and District Otterhounds in the early 1860s, enjoying popularity and much success for the next two decades. I believe it was this chap who greatly influenced Jim Dalton and helped shape his ideas regarding terrier breeding. Jim Dalton was one of the first to begin using good quality fox terriers in order to produce typey, game earth dogs that were found at the Blencathra during his reign. It was during Sanderson's time at this hunt that great terriers, fox terriers bred from Parson Russell's original strain, were bred and worked and these had a massive impact on Lake District terrier strains from this time on.

During this era, otterhounds often met at 6am in order to pick up a fresh drag at the first opportunity and long hard days were then had on the river, with epic walks back to kennels once hunting was over. It was a hard life and could be considered as only a little easier than that of a fell pack Huntsman.

Thunder was one of the Carlisle and District's best otterhounds during Sanderson's time at the hunt and one day he led the pack from Newby Bridge, only a few miles from kennels, taking the drag for several miles until, at last, their otter was found

The Dallam Tower otterhounds, also known as the Kendal & District (c.1910).

about Corby Castle, the place after which Corby, one of Joe Bowman's best fox-killing terriers at the end of the nineteenth century, was named. A two-hour hunt then followed and a large otter of almost 30lbs was eventually killed on the river. Hounds were kennelled at Canal Bank, close to the river Eden, and they covered a massive area, often going into the Lake District itself, particularly around Ullswater. The Dumfriesshire Otterhounds were another pack which hunted into the Lake District and Billy Scott proved a popular Huntsman of that famous establishment.

I think I can safely say that more otters were accounted for in the Lake District than in any other hunted county of England. But despite this, I do not believe it was hunting that caused such a catastrophic decline in their numbers in the 1960s and 70s. Poison and pollution have now been blamed for the near-decimation of the English otter at this time.

Those involved in otter hunting were invariably very keen on otters and so, when otters disappeared suddenly from our waterways, the packs voluntarily gave up hunting them.

Subsequently, otters became a protected species and it is now totally illegal to hunt them. More otters escaped during the days of the otter hunt, however, than were caught. Otters, in fact, were one of the more difficult creatures to account for and mostly only old and sick individuals fell to hounds and terriers. Healthy otters were incredibly quick and could endure long hunts along the rivers without difficulty, so most did get away. The odds were certainly in the otter's favour when being hunted.

Polecat and pinemarten hunts

Close cousins of the otter are the polecat and the pinemarten and both were once heavily hunted in the fells in order to claim bounties on their carcasses, or tails. And packs of hounds, with a few terriers included, were the most effective way of finding and catching such quarry. In the early days, though, guns and traps were also employed, as such quarry as these could so easily escape by getting into rocky lairs from where it was impossible to get at them. Both were simply known as Marts, so it is impossible to know which was being hunted when one comes across rare accounts describing a mart hunt.

Polecats, though, were known as foulmarts, or foumarts, because of their rank stench — a result of scent glands used for territorial purposes, or to put off any pursuers game enough to take them on (this stench was designed to tell predators that, as a food source, they would taste as bad as they smelt! This would then put the predator off, but not a hunting dog). Pinemartens were known as sweetmarts, and they gave grand hunts. Hounds held pinemarten scent well and would enjoy some long runs.

What was needed for hunting marts were a few hounds that could stick to a line and cross the country with noses almost constantly to the ground; and the old type of heavily built, slow-hunting harrier was ideal for this activity. Run a brace or two of terriers with such hounds and one had the perfect ingredients for success. And this is exactly how those hunters of old sought out their polecats and pinemartens. The hounds provided the necessary nose, whilst the terriers provided the necessary speed, which was essential once the quarry had been located. Both species of mart bolted at great speed and pace was essential.

Both polecats and pinemartens left a strong scent that hounds loved to follow and very cold drags could be taken up. In fact, legend has it that many a hunt began at a pile of rocks, went on to cover sometimes several miles, then ended up back at the original rockpiles, where hounds now marked. Another legend tells of a hunt in John Peel country when hounds marked a rocky

Followers of otterhounds at St John's in the Vale.

lair near Isel. This pack, in fact, may well have been Peel's own. Terriers immediately got in among the rocks and with a little help from diggers with crowbars, a polecat quickly bolted and was either shot, or was taken by hounds and terriers. The hounds then picked up a 'new' line and raced away as one, with scent taking them for several miles nearly all the way to Cockermouth, before turning sharply and going all the way back to where they had just killed. It was unusual to kill first and then hunt the scent, but, with mart hunting, anything could happen, as hounds could take up a drag that was many hours old.

Marts were usually hunted at first light. Most of the fell packs continued to hunt such quarry well into the twentieth century, though rarely as a main quarry by the end of the nineteenth century, by which time foxes had taken over from hares as the principal quarry. Unlike in other parts of the country, there is no evidence to suggest there were any packs used exclusively for polecats and pinemartens, as such were usually hunted when found, or if a mart drag was taken up.

Hares, foxes, badgers, polecats, pinemartens and stoats – all were hunted in those days and bounties claimed on those accounted for. Even deer were hunted and the carted deer was employed by some packs, even that owned by John Peel, as we have already seen. Bagged foxes were also hunted at times, but rarely, and this practise was never popular in the fells. Bagged foxes were used quite regularly by some southern outfits, but very few Lake District packs had any interest in such artificial hunting and any bagged foxes occasionally hunted were wild ones saved from hounds during a previous hunt and re-released early on the morning of their next outing, a cruel and rarely-seen practise in the fells.

But mart-hunting was done naturally and for the sake of control of a predator, though the bounty scheme did move some to overdo things and large numbers were killed, especially by keepers who kept a hound or two of their own, together with a brace of terriers.

Polecats and pinemartens often got into tricky borrans from which they just couldn't be extracted and so they had to be left, but the Cumbrian race – a mix of Viking and Celtic blood in the main – were determined hunters and dug out ('grubbed') their quarry if at all possible, efforts which sometimes took a day or two, even longer on occasion.

Cold scents of polecats in particular could be followed by any moderately experienced pack of hounds, and yet another account tells of hounds being loosed from kennels, possibly from Peel's own buildings. And from that very farmyard they immediately took up a drag which led them for several miles out onto the Caldbeck Fells and almost to Skiddaw, before they turned and hunted all the way back home, with the polecat then being found back at the very farmyard where the hounds were housed. Their quarry was flushed out after a bit of effort and was accounted for.

Hounds marking an otter holt.

Otterhounds drawing for scent, looking for a drag.

Polecats became extinct in many areas by the Second World War though it is very unlikely that this was the case in the county of Cumbria. There are such strongholds in this area that accounting for every animal, even with the use of guns, traps and dogs, would be impossible and I think it certain that a few held on and that these, meeting up, and mating with escaped ferrets left down rabbit holes by their owners, then went on to populate the Lake District once more.

Polecats will probably never again be found in such large numbers as they reached during the nineteenth century when they were a popular quarry species for some packs. Locators now mean that most ferrets can be retrieved after killing rabbits below ground, but before locators arrived on the scene during the latter part of the twentieth century, lost ferrets were quite common and it is these that have definitely aided the recovery of polecat numbers.

◇◇◇◇◇◇◇◇◇

10

HOUNDS & TERRIERS
OF THE LAKE DISTRICT

Fellhounds are quite different to foxhounds found working with mounted packs and this difference is undoubtedly due to the recent addition of running dog blood, possibly greyhound, or greyhound-lurchers, that has given fellhounds a lighter bone and that bit of extra speed. Mounted packs that hunt open country such as the Zetland and College Valley, often use fellhound blood as an outcross in order to give that bit of extra speed that can be lacking in packs of shire foxhounds. Speed was once less important than scenting ability and in any case the fox was shot, or dug out, when located. As the nineteenth century progressed, hunting the fox becoming more important, and more hound speed was required. There is no doubt that the hounds of the fells have become progressively faster in recent years. This has been due to selective modern breeding.

Good nose and bone structure have also been qualities aimed at in fell country breeding programmes and there can be no doubt that Welsh and English Foxhound blood has played a major part in this. Although fellhounds must be lighter of bone in order to provide speed and agility when working rough country they must also have good strong legs that can stand several seasons working amongst crags and boulder-strewn country that would very quickly weed out weakly specimens. And so there was no compromise on bone structure. Some argue that many of the shire packs have bred too much bone into their hounds and this undoubtedly accounts for the sad fact that many of those hounds can only work for around five seasons before being retired. Fellhounds, on the other hand, can go on working for as many as nine or ten seasons in many cases and this is definitely due to lighter bone and a much freer movement than can be found amongst more heavily-boned hounds. However, many have come to this realisation and have used fellhound blood in order to improve on bone structure.

Welsh blood was used to some extent (Willie Irving records that Welsh Hound blood went into the breeding of the Melbreak during the early decades of the twentieth century) and occasional fellhounds have been born with some roughness to their coats over the years, which is a throwback to the Welsh Hound. Also, such a cross was thought to have improved the hound's independent behaviour which is essential in mountainous terrain, where hounds are often left to work out a line alone and unaided. A large proportion of a hunt would, in fact, be carried out without anybody nearby, so fell-hounds had to be able to put themselves right whenever they checked (lost the scent).

The Welsh Hound was famed for its independent spirit and ability to work out a line unaided, but it also had a great scenting skill that fell hunters found most attractive. This was yet another reason why Welsh strains were brought into fellhound bloodlines. Occasional foxhound crosses have been brought into the fell strains in order to improve bone, whenever it was getting a little too light; and a good nose was also kept by using such outcross blood.

All this mixing has resulted in a unique type of hound that hunts cold drag superbly, finds well and sticks to a line once a hunt gets going, with hounds putting themselves right whenever things get a little difficult. Also, fellhounds possess great intelligence and so, when a fox was to climb a crag, they could work

Jim Dalton's famous Blencathra Turk (1910).

out in their own minds which was the best route to approach it and this was a spectacular sight. They would also fan out whilst drawing, covering a wide area of the fell-side, and all would come together once a drag had been struck, or a fox roused. Hounds would nearly burst their hearts getting back together on a drag and the sight of a pack hunting a fox round a crag, or across a rough fell-side was indeed a sight to behold.

Great intelligence also meant that these fellhounds could find their way home over long distances, some missing for days before finding their way back to kennels, or to the place where they had been walked since puppyhood. Hound walkers generally walk the same hounds each summer, which provides stability to what are sensitive animals who would not thrive if they were pushed from pillar to post.

The fellhound is truly a superb hunting animal that has been used to improve the working ability of several packs in several different countries, including America. It has been necessary to have excellent hounds for hunting the incredibly rough, mountainous landscape that makes up much of the Lake District, but it can accurately be said that without game terriers to bring up the rear, so to speak, then hunting with hounds alone would be rendered most ineffectual.

Fell terriers

Earth-stopping in fell terrain where huge rocky strongholds are the underground domain of the foxes, has usually been impossible. So it has been vital to breed agile, game terriers who can stand hours of walking on the mountains in often-freezing conditions. And, after this, they need to be able to withstand

High Lea Laddie (c.1929), grandsire of Gypsy of Melbreak and precursor of the modern fell terrier.

long stints below ground, either attempting to bolt a fox, stay with it until dug out, or kill it in the earth. At one time, hunting in the fells was about fox control, not 'sport', so foxes could not be left for another day if they refused to bolt. They could not so easily be dug out either and many earths are so rocky or so deep, they are utterly impossible to dig, so a terrier had to be game enough to tackle and kill a fox that wouldn't bolt, and then have enough strength left to get out of the depths of the earth.

A baying type of terrier was often put into an earth first because their noise was most likely to bolt the fox. But, if the fox refused to shift and the Huntsman and landowner wanted it destroyed, then a hard terrier was put in. It is said that 'hard' terriers rarely made good finders in these often-vast earths, but that simply isn't true. The fact is that harder terriers rarely got a chance to find because a 'baying' type had already been put in first in order to attempt to bolt the fox.

There were exceptions to this rule, however, such as when it was late in the day and the Huntsman didn't require the fox to be bolted, or when the hunted beast was a lamb, or poultry, killer. But in general these baying types often gained great reputations as finders, while the harder terriers gained great reputations for their skill at killing immovable foxes underground. Joe Wear's famous Tear 'Em was one such hard terrier with a great reputation for killing foxes and he, along with a select few such as Anthony Barker's Rock and Bowman's Corby and Fury, killed three foxes in one day's hunting.

Tear 'Em's finest hour

It was during the late 1940s that the Ullswater hounds had a game fox afoot and they hunted it across the bleak fell-tops, with a screaming scent keeping the pack in full cry, until their quarry, pressed severely by the relentless pack, finally went to ground in a large rocky lair near Troutbeck. Joe Wear entered Tear 'Em, which suggests he required the fox to be killed, rather than bolted, and a battle royal almost immediately broke out underground. Leaving the fighting pair, Wear now moved on to try for another, leaving his Whipper-in, Tom Robinson, along with John Pool, to attend to things at the earth. Robinson and Pool dug as fast as they possibly could and after some time and effort they finally broke through, coming upon Tear 'Em just as he had finished off a large fox. Incredibly, after further examination, a total of three foxes were discovered lying stone dead inside that earth and, amazingly, Tear 'Em was scarcely bitten during that fierce encounter!

This famous Ullswater terrier was owned by Jim 'Gillie' Fleming of Grasmere. Tear 'Em was a son of Myrt (bred by Willie Irving and sold to Fleming about 1938) and Ullswater Rock. Ullswater Rock had served with this famous pack during Anthony Barker's time at the hunt when the Second World War was raging and he was yet another who was used to kill reluctant foxes. Rock was incredibly hard and could kill any fox that refused to shift for a baying terrier which Barker had sent in to bolt his fox. It was Rock who sired Anthony Barker's Judy and Willie Irving's Jim, these two terriers being out of the same litter as Tear 'Em (see *Willie Irving: Terrierman, Huntsman and Lakelander*). Judy became the Grandam of Barker's famous Rock, who sired Sid Wilkinson's Rock – possibly the most potent sire of several dynasties of modern working Fell and Lakeland terriers.

Many of the later Huntsmen used this system of trying to bolt, rather than kill, foxes, though earlier Huntsmen seem to have used hard terriers in the earths in the main. Even the hard bitch terriers were fox killers, though on many occasions foxes were bolted to the waiting pack. Willie Irving certainly used hard terriers in the main. The Eskdale and Ennerdale terriers were mostly hard too, so Irving probably adopted the system he learnt from Willie Porter during his formative years spent with that hunt. The Blencathra also specialised in hard fox killers, noteably under Jim Dalton, who infused his terrier strain with game fox terrier blood that had seen service at all large quarry.

The Blencathra hounds eager to be loosed.

In those days several fox terriers were 'hard' types, rather than 'bayers', and such qualities were passed onto their offspring. That hard blood is still found in Fell, Lakeland and Patterdale terrier strains of today. It should be added that some terriers begin their careers as baying types, but develop into hard fox killers over time.

Maxie

One of the hardest terriers to see service with a fell pack was Maxie; a big powerful Lakeland dog bred out of Eric Dobson's 'N Beck' strain of working Lakeland terrier. Such terriers were bred out of Harry Hardisty, Cyril Tyson, and the Oregill Lakeland bloodlines belonging to Alan Johnston (grandson of Alf Johnston). Other traditional West Lakeland bloodlines went back to the famous 'typey' terriers belonging to Willie, Harry and Arthur Irving.

Maxie would kill any fox that refused to bolt, but he was a quarrelsome terrier and often had a go at the hounds! Arthur Irving continued to hunt with the Eskdale and Ennerdale pack long after he had retired as Huntsman and still kept his strain of pedigree Lakelands and he used them with hounds when the opportunity arose. In fact, Art was more keen on terriers than on hounds and he bred some great game stock, all of which were descended from Willie Irving's Melbreak strain. Art warned the owner of Maxie to keep his belligerent tyke away from the hounds, but the game terrier continued to show them aggression whenever he got the chance.

One day the Eskdale and Ennerdale pack were marking a rock earth on the fell-side and Maxie was released into the earth. The terrier disappeared round a rocky corner in search of the best way to his fox, all the while bristling with fury and indignation as he pushed his way through the eager pack. All of a sudden there was a loud and fierce commotion which indicated

The Blencathra hounds on the trail in John Peel country.

that hounds finally had had enough of this aggressive little tyke. Maxie's owner was quickly on the spot only to discover that Arthur's warnings had been prophetic. There was nothing left of the terrier but a small patch of skin and fur!

Red Ike

Another grand working terrier who could finish any fox that wouldn't bolt was Albert Benson's Red Ike; one of the ancestors of most modern Fell and Patterdale terriers. For years I was unable to find any photographs of this terrier, but believe I have at last discovered one. The photo (see page 17) shows Albert Benson in the mid-1930s at a meet in Borrowdale, gathering at the *Borrowdale Hotel*, with a group of terriers at his feet. Ike was red, an Irish leggy terrier, standing taller than the other Blencathra terriers. He was also full of fire and extremely eager to work. The terrier with the white blaze, coupled in the foreground, exactly fits the description of Red Ike. He is obviously taller than the rest by a good inch or two, exactly resembling an old

Blencathra hounds resting after an exhausting day on Carrock.

fashioned Irish terrier. His jacket is harsh and tight and this terrier, as can be discerned from the photo, had much presence. No other Blencathra terrier at the time fits the description of this dog. Ike served several bitches during his time at both the Blencathra and Coniston Foxhounds. Ike was put into service with Coniston Whipper-in Anthony Chapman after Benson left the Blencathra in 1937.

Immigrant terriers

Mining, quarrying, road laying, professional pest control, farm work and walling all brought immigrant workers into the Lake District and many of these brought their game terriers with them. Irish stock has played a massive part in the development of English earth dog breeds and the fell strains too had more than their fair share of such bloodlines. Welsh terriers have also played a large part, as well as fox and Bedlington terrier strains. Other outcross blood has come from Scottish breeds and this rich mix produced the Fell and the Patterdale terriers (Patterdale terriers were given the name of Lakeland terriers in 1912) for which the Lake District has become famous. Border terriers sprang from a similar mix and these are very closely related to the old fell strains. The Lakeland terrier became more carefully bred after 1912, as before this time much of the breeding was based on putting the gamest dog to the gamest bitch. This invariably produced a good temperament but it didn't always produce sound stock that could both work intelligently, and stand up to the rigours of hunting mountainous country.

The breeder Douglas Paisley, from Whitehaven, used Border terriers during the latter part of the nineteenth century, but when he first started hunting with the Blencathra Foxhounds he began to find them inferior to the Lakeland terrier stock.

Paisley was particularly impressed by a bitch called Wasp,

An old photograph of fox terriers in the 1920s, of the type used to improve the strain of the Lakeland terriers.

probably one of Dalton's terriers that may have been descended, in part at least, from fox terriers working with the Carlisle & District Otterhounds. Dalton hunted with this pack during the summer, and it sometimes had joint meets with the Blencathra when the foxhunting and otterhunting seasons overlapped.

So the Blencathra and the Carlisle & District Otterhounds would sometimes meet together at the start of a day, and then Dalton would take his hounds to the fells, whilst the otterhounds took to the rivers and becks. Wasp so impressed Paisley that he founded his future strain on her and all his later stock can be traced back to her. She was so good, in fact, that he decided to abandon Border terriers altogether and from then on bred only from Lakeland terrier stock. Wasp was probably one of the ancestors of Jim Dalton's famous Turk.

Douglas Paisley became a top breeder of good looking, extremely game Lakeland terriers and he was also a very well-respected judge, having enjoyed great success in the show ring and at Kennel Club shows. In fact, he was one of the first exhibitors to appear at Kennel Club shows in 1928 when the first classes were staged and he also enjoyed the most success. Tom Meagean of Whitehaven, however, soon took over as winner of most terrier titles, though most if his stock were bred by Alf Johnston and Willie Irving, with Kitchen, Gibbons, Long and a few other noted breeders also supplying him with terriers.

Professional exhibitors such as Meagean eventually dominated the terrier show world and hunting folk like Bruce and Paisley quickly became disillusioned with exhibiting and stopped attending shows. As early as the beginning of the 1940s, Paisley

Douglas Paisley with pedigree Lakelands which served at the Blencathra Hunt.

used his terriers for work only, though he continued to exhibit at hunt shows staged throughout the fell country. He also continued to judge, though working qualities were all-important with him, such as those about to be discussed.

Working qualities

The Lakeland terrier was actually designed by hunters for working in the fells. Dalton, Paisley, Bruce, Irving; all helped to shape this new type of fell terrier and every quality they sought, excepting colour, was with work in mind. Narrow shoulders meant easier negotiation of tight passages and narrow crag ledges. A height of no more than fifteen inches meant these terriers

An early LTA Show near Keswick (Skiddaw in background). Tom Meagean holding his Lakeland terrier (first competitor on left).

could get into most earths, as long as they had narrow chests too. A certain amount of legginess was sought so that the terriers could negotiate rough ground and have enough leg-length to jump on and off rock ledges.

This was illustrated in an article written by Mrs Spence many years ago in which she mentions a Neville Dawson who was a friend of Kitty Farrer, the Ullswater Foxhounds Secretary at the time. Farrer lived at Howtown and he looked after two of Dawson's terriers for a time, one a Lakeland and the other a Scottish terrier.

The pair went off hunting together and only one – the Lakeland – returned to Farrer's home. The terrier was restless and Farrer followed the dog up a nearby fell to where he could hear barking inside a rock hole.

The Scottish terrier couldn't get out, so Farrer dug down to a ledge, underneath which was the terrier and the now very dead fox. The pair had killed their fox and the Lakeland was able to jump onto the ledge and get out, but the Scottie, having much shorter legs couldn't follow and would have died in that earth had the Lakeland not led Farrer to the spot. This experience demonstrates how important a bit of leg length can be for terriers working rocky country.

Conformation of the terrier

Straight legs in terriers (as opposed to bow-legs) were also sought because foxes had straight legs and this seemed to help their agility. Straight legs would certainly help when it came to flushing foxes from narrow crag ledges, as they were often called upon to do.

Bow-legs often went hand-in-hand with broad shoulders in a terrier, and this conformation was not suitable for narrow ledges.

Coarse, thick 'jackets' were also required on Lakeland

terriers (the poor-coated Bedlington types suffered a lot during inclement weather). A waterproof, windproof coat was much the best. So, in the fells, only really hard-coated terriers were bred and, in time, an almost impenetrable jacket was achieved that kept the worst of the weather at bay. Such a coat held off much of the icy water and mud found in peat earths in particular, notoriously bad places for chilling and killing a working terrier sent in to bolt or kill, a hunted fox.

Also, such a hard jacket helped when terriers were sent into dense bramble and gorse coverts where hounds couldn't penetrate. Terriers, in fact, are descended from small hounds that were originally used for flushing game from undergrowth that wouldn't allow larger hounds access. Just watch a terrier pack at work and you will quickly see hound qualities coming out in them.

Good bone structure was also necessary and strong heads, with powerful, punishing jaws were sought. A powerful scissor-bite was also important. Level, overshot or undershot mouths were regarded as breeding faults.

Hunts in more recent times have placed much more on bolting the foxes; but before the Second World War it was the norm to have Lakelands that would kill any fox that didn't bolt very swiftly. Most Lakelands had sense enough not to get too badly knocked about, though a fox in a commanding position would sometimes badly maul its foe.

On rare occasions a terrier would die from such wounds, usually because there were no antibiotics in those days and wounds could get badly infected. Willie Irving does record though, that a few of his game terriers did have their mouths 'spoiled' by bad maulings, especially when they came up against badgers found lurking where a fox had gone to ground. A previously 'perfect' mouth could be rendered undershot or even overshot, by severe maulings.

On a few occasions Irving's terriers bolted, or killed, their fox, then turned their attentions to a badger skulking in the same earth. Willie would always have to dig them out on these occasions and the terriers were usually badly mauled as a result of the encounter.

Sense was rated highly in fell terriers by Huntsmen of Irving's ilk and their terriers could mostly kill a fox without receiving anything other than minor bites, but such tactics didn't pay off with badgers and a terrier was invariably badly injured when encountering such a powerful adversary.

Tragedy strikes

No matter what qualities were bred into terriers working in the fells, there were times when the forces of nature were just too powerful for them and this was illustrated one day when the Blencathra pack ran a fox to ground on the Rigg, not far from Threlkeld where hounds are still kennelled today. Dalton put in one of his best terriers, probably sired by his famous Turk.

It was late in the day and Dalton wanted the fox killed, so in went the terrier and, sure enough, it quickly found and engaged its fox. Dusk descended rapidly, as it does during the winter months, and so the Huntsman was forced to leave his terrier in overnight, though he knew it would make its way back to kennels if it got out during the hours of darkness. But his terrier didn't return to kennels during the night, so Dalton was on the spot at first light the next day.

There had been a heavy frost and the land was gripped in ice, the ground rendered as hard as iron. The terrier had killed its fox and had drawn it out of the earth, which was a peculiar quirk found in quite a few of the early Lakelands, but the encounter and effort of pulling its victim out of the narrow rock lair had left the terrier so weak that it was forced to lie down and had been overcome by the freezing temperatures. Dalton found his gallant terrier stone dead, its frozen body next to that of its victim.

Another sad loss was in January 1934 when the Coniston pack hunted a fox in the Langdale area and eventually ran their quarry to ground at a place called Cat Lugs. Three terriers were put into what looked like an average sort of rock hole, but this lair proved a dangerous one and the terriers became trapped. A

A white Lakeland in 1946.

long dig ensued with several followers assisting.

After an incredible six long and tiring days, during which tons of rock were unearthed, a terrier bitch called Spider, was successfully rescued. The moment she was lifted from the lair was caught on camera and can be seen in the photograph included on page 122. This is a wonderfully atmospheric scene that has captured the joy one feels when rescuing a trapped tyke. Sadly, the other two terriers were never seen again.

The Lake District is a hard country that has taken a heavy toll on the lives of hounds and terriers. Crags, deep borrans, swollen becks and, in more modern times some fast roads, have all played a part in making working the fells one of the most heart-breaking hunt countries on the planet. However, such tragedies are still quite rare when compared to the number of hunting days during an average season. A hard country indeed, but one of the best for seeing great hound work and for seeing some of the gamest of terriers to be found anywhere.

11

◇◇◇◇◇◇◇◇

HUNTING THE FELLS TODAY

The Hunting Act came into force in February 2005. Basically it dictates that only two hounds can be used for flushing foxes towards waiting guns. If a pack is to go out hunting, then either rats, rabbits, or artificial scent is to be the quarry. This has made things very difficult for the fell packs, though, at the time of writing, all are still operating and all enjoy great support from farmers, local communities and visitors. The actual hunting is not the same as it was, of course, and there is always that feeling of oppression that comes from being subjected to an unjust, prejudiced law. But hunting continues and the fells lend themselves to spectacular views of hound work.

Trail hunting

A trail of scent can be laid, either using aniseed, or scent made from the bodies of foxes flushed and shot in order to control their numbers, though it is not easy retraining hounds to hunt such 'quarry', especially the older hounds. To hunt anything other than live scent, hounds must be entered (ie. start hunting) young, at about six or seven months of age, when curiosity means they are trying every bit of smell that comes their way, and they must get a reward at the end of it.

Fellhounds can compete alongside trail hounds, although they are usually a bit stronger, slower and stockier. Sometimes, their strength and stamina can prevail against the swifter trail

Barry Todhunter still gathering his hounds after a long day on the hill.

hounds. Fell-sides the whole length of a valley can be trailed, providing splendid views of the hounds for foot and car followers alike. If entered early, then hounds should also speak (bay) to trailed scent, though some will not speak as keenly as they will to live quarry.

Trying to keep hunting within the law is essential, though foxes will always be disturbed and hounds will occasionally switch to a fox when trail hunting out on the fells. It is utterly impossible to prevent this. The trail layer will often accidentally lead the pack past a fox lying low, and when hounds approach, or even if Reynard hears the hunting horn in the distance, he will often make a move. His 'live' scent can be picked up by hounds from even long distances from where a fox has risen and gone away and then one can do nothing to stop hounds getting onto the line and going off in hot pursuit.

Out on the fells, a Huntsman cannot get in front of his pack to stop them and so he can do little to prevent a hunt from occurring. The law allows for such accidental hunting, provided there was no intention to hunt such live quarry. If a trail is put down and hounds laid on, then one cannot be accused of intending to hunt live quarry, though many Huntsmen find it is best to take video footage, even if only on a mobile phone, of the trail being laid.

The actual line remains a secret to the Huntsman and followers, in order to keep some excitement and anticipation. The trail layer himself, or an assistant, can easily take footage of the start of the trail and this could be saved on computer disc with appropriate times and dates also being recorded. The antis are using videos in order to try to get hunting folk prosecuted, so why not beat them at their own game?

There has been much uncertainty over whether or not the cold scent of a fox can be followed by a pack of hounds, as this can aid the location of a fox, especially that of a lamb, poultry, or gamebird killer. Once the location is found, as hounds approach a likely spot, they could be stopped and two hounds sent in to flush the quarry, with a gun or two in place to shoot the fox. The case against Tony Wright of the Exmoor Foxhounds, which was won by the accused, has given a precedent in law and this case settled the issue of following a cold drag: if an animal is not aware of being hunted, then hounds following a cold drag from the previous night cannot be said to be hunting. Any such hound work is therefore exempt from the hunting act, as long as the intent is to stop hounds at a likely covert and flush the quarry using two hounds only, and to have a gun waiting to account for the fox, if a safe and clean shot is possible.

This case also showed that accidental hunting is not illegal: if hounds get away on a fox, then such hunting is exempt from the act, provided there was no intent.

Hounds heading for the Fells.

This method of controlling foxes with a waiting gun does have its risks, and more so in the fells than anywhere else. The sheer volume of rocks, for instance, makes ricochet of even shotgun pellets more likely, which could compromise the safety of both hounds and followers. Also, the fells contain large numbers of walkers all year round and there could be some safety issues because of this. Certainly, such legislation has made it more difficult to carry out fox control in mountainous districts and these areas are where fox control is more necessary.

Cold drag is simply an old scent trail; it is not the hot scent of a beast roused from covert and pursued across country. Trail hunting is legal and surely hunting cold drag comes under this category! Using this method would keep a pack working well together and, on approach of a likely spot, two hounds could be sent on and guns posted in suitable places, with the flushed fox being shot only when it was entirely safe to do so. The carcass could then be dragged across the fell-side for a good distance and the pack laid on again. Hunting drag means that the cold drag of a lamb-killing fox can now be followed to a likely spot where two hounds can be used for flushing to guns.

A warm carcass will leave a good scent and this trail will be eagerly hunted by hounds. I have used this method trail hunting myself with a pack of terriers. Terriers were originally small hounds and they are still capable of holding to the line of a fox. Several of the fell pack terriers have at times broken away and gone off hunting with hounds, and on numerous occasions it has been confirmed by followers that the terrier was actually leading hounds!

A Blencathra Hunt report, for instance, tells of a terrier leading hounds as they hunted their fox over the fell-tops into Lorton Vale. Terriers will hunt a warm trail as eagerly as if the fox were alive. This is possible only while the carcass remains warm, which gives the trail layer about half an hour, possibly a

A 2008 meet at Mungrisedale.

little longer. There is nothing one can do with the carcass of a shot fox, so why not use it immediately after shooting for the purposes of laying a trail?

In the final analysis, Governments cannot legislate against natural law and it is natural for dogs to hunt and kill foxes. This occurs in the wild, with packs of wolves, jackals, coyote and other wild dogs, so any attempts to stop hounds from following their instincts are simply futile. Courts should remember this when handling any cases of alleged illegal hunting!

It has been claimed that it is not actually illegal for hounds to hunt a fox, but it is illegal to follow them whilst doing so. But one has to follow hounds in order to know where they are, in order to attempt to stop them.

Or should the Huntsman and followers simply leave hounds to get on with it, not bothering about busy roads, railway lines and other dangers that may be encountered, just to avoid breaking this ridiculous and unworkable ruling?

Meanwhile, though, the fell packs try to keep within current legislation, even if the odds are stacked against their attempts to hunt within the law, and to rely on exemptions from the Act whenever hounds do get away on live quarry.

Drag hunting continues, some using scent from the rotting carcasses of dead foxes that have been flushed and shot quite legally, while others use artificial scents. One pack I know of cooks liver and then leaves it standing for a day or two to increase the smell. They then place the liver in a container of water mixed with vegetable oil, or just vegetable oil alone, and

Turk of Melbreak, winning again in 1932.

this creates the scent for the trail. Hounds will hunt it quite well, even speaking to the line, though not as well as when live quarry is hunted. If young hounds take eagerly to such scent, then older ones may be induced to join in, though the older hounds don't seem to have the same eagerness as youngsters entered at about six or seven months of age.

If things become too difficult for the Huntsmen of the fell packs, because of foxes literally 'getting up' anywhere, then following human scent in the same manner as do bloodhound packs would be another option. Entering foxhounds to this method would not be as easy as entering bloodhounds, true, though it can be done.

I once entered a young lurcher that was part beagle-bred to human scent and I managed to teach it to stick to a line – a lesson it learnt well when later hunting rabbits, hares and foxes. Young six-month-old fellhounds could be entered to human scent without too much difficulty by giving them an item of clothing that belongs to the 'runner' and allowing hounds to quickly find them at first, being rewarded with treats and much praise. The hunts can then be extended and a human 'runner' used on the fells.

This form of hunting is the next best thing to real live quarry hunting and I am certain the Huntsmen of bloodhound packs would willingly give advice to the fell packs about entering to human scent. In this way, a portion of the pack could be used for this form of hunting, while another portion could be used for fox control within the hunting act.

Terrier work has also been restricted by the current hunting ban and now one can only use one at a time underground at any one time; and then only if they are being used for the protection of gamebirds, or wild birds that are nurtured for shooting purposes. More baffling legislation does not exist! Why can terriers be used for bolting foxes to guns in order to protect gamebirds, but the shepherd who has lambs killed, or the farmer who loses poultry, cannot? Let us hope that sense eventually prevails and a licensing scheme comes into operation that allows both hound and terrier work for the purposes of pest control.

A lot of ground is keepered in the Lake District, so terrier work, as long as written permission is obtained and carried on one's person, continues. Only one terrier can be put in an earth at any one time, and if one uses a youngster alongside a more experienced adult terrier for flushing from covert, then that youngster will enter very naturally when it begins earth work.

Terriers used for flushing are fulfilling the original task for which they were bred and so such work is every bit as important as work carried out below ground. And, believe me, it takes a good finder to locate and shift a fox from a dense covert.

Foot followers

Following hounds on foot is very rewarding indeed, though one must use common sense and be well equipped for the mountains, which, in winter, are often subject to arctic weather. Warm waterproof clothing is essential. Clothing should ideally be lightweight and there is no need to be weighed down with bulging rucksacks. A good pair of walking boots is essential. Willie Irving used to coat his boots with grease from the kennels' boiler and this certainly worked well. Ankle supports are essential as the ground can be very rough. A good stout stick, of the shepherd's crook variety, will also be useful, especially climbing out to the fell-tops.

The best views are from the tops, though stick to the low country if it is misty and try to keep with regular followers who will be only too happy to give you advice so that you stay safe.

And, if mist is coming on, descend to a lower level in order to keep out of it. If the mist becomes very dense, then hunting will probably be cancelled. If you do not know the area, carry a compass and an ordnance survey map covering that particular district, though this is not necessary if you keep with locals. Never go onto the fells without food and drink and, along with sandwiches, I would advise that you take some fruit, for slow energy release, and a rapid energiser such as Kendal Mint Cake, or chocolate. Carry a mobile phone and before setting out, make certain that it has enough credit and is fully charged, in case of emergencies. Problems are incredibly rare among followers of fell packs, though one must still make certain that all has been done to stay as safe as possible.

Car followers

Car followers need to apply only common sense too. Never drive along whilst looking up at the fell-sides for hounds. Always stop

The next generation of Lunesdale puppies (1974).

Hunting in the Lake District: the views can be awesome! Digging out an otter in the 1920s.

first and pull in off the road, making sure there is enough room for other vehicles to pass. If hounds approach a road, then use your hazard lights to slow down traffic and assist followers who try to stop hounds. Car followers are invaluable in such circumstances as they can stop hounds, or at the very least slow down traffic so that hounds can cross safely if they cannot be stopped.

Finally, whether on foot, or following by car, a good pair of binoculars will come in most useful and great hound work can then be enjoyed from long distances. I would urge anybody of reasonable health and agility to go fell hunting in the Lake District and to enjoy the wonderful air and scenery, as well as the superb work of a pack of fellhounds. All of this is to be found among the mountains of Cumbria. Following a fell pack is a great form of exercise!

Whatever methods are employed in order to keep hounds and terriers working in Cumbria and, most importantly, in order to provide a pest control service for farmers and keepers alike, it is important that folk continue to fully support local traditions and to keep hunting in the fells as part of Lake District life. Hunting in the fells is an integral part of that awesome, fear-inspiring and enchanting part of the world. And long may we sing:

"Hark forrard, good hounds, tally ho."